ROYAL CANADIAN MOUNTED POLICE

ROYAL CANADIAN MOUNTED POLICE

By Richard L. Neuberger

Illustrated by Lee J. Ames

Random House · New York

For

MAURINE

*Who went on patrol and baked the famous
chocolate cake just as good as the
Mountie's wife!*

Contents

1   Canada—The Land the Mounties Patrol   3

2   "The Finest Police Force in the World!"   13

3   To Uphold the Right   32

4   "Stamix Otokon" Makes Peace with the Indians   45

5   The Mounties Show the Railroad the Way   61

6   The Wilderness Police and the Gold Rush   79

7   The Patrol That Never Came Back   96

8   Tracking Down an Arctic Mystery   110

9   The Mounties Conquer the Northwest Passage   129

10   The Streamlined Mounties of Today   145

11   Some Mounties Who Are Friends of Mine   165

A Few Thanks

EITHER THROUGH PERSONAL FRIENDSHIP OR BY INFORMA-tion officially supplied, many members of the Royal Canadian Mounted Police have helped me to write this book.

I should like especially to voice my debt to Commissioner L. H. Nicholson, former Commissioner Stuart Taylor Wood, Assistant Commissioner Alan T. Belcher, Assistant Commissioner E. C. Rivett-Carnac, the late Assistant Commissioner C. D. La Nauze, Superintendent George J. Archer, Superintendent H. P. Mathewson, the late Super-intendent H. H. Cronkhite, Inspector R. A. S. MacNeil, Inspector E. S. W. Batty, Inspector Henry A. Larsen, Inspector H. J. Spanton, ex-Inspector William Grennan, Sergeant Barry Allen, Sergeant John Piper, Constable George Fleming and Mr. George T. Hann, who served as Departmental Secretary of the force for twenty-nine years.

For the information I have given about Canada gener-ally I am grateful to Dr. Charles Camsell, Premier Ernest C. Manning, Dr. Hugh L. Keenleyside, Harry Rowed, Richard Finnie, R. D. McLean, Ernest Evans, George G. Vincent and Harry J. Jomini of the Aluminum Company of Canada, B. A. McKelvie of the *Vancouver Province*, J. Hugh Campbell and Graham Nichols of the Canadian Pacific Railway, George S. Towill of the Canadian National Railway, J. Aubrey Simmons and E. T. Applewhaite of the Canadian House of Commons, to the late Joseph Kinsey Howard, to the late Alec Hunter of the *Prince Rupert Daily News* and to Corporal H. E. Brownhill, editor of the *Royal Canadian Mounted Police Quarterly*.

That I have been able to see so much of the Mounted Police work in the Canadian North Country was due mainly to the challenging assignments given me by my two wartime commanding officers in the United States Army—the late General James A. O'Connor and Colonel (now General) Kenneth B. Bush.

To all these people I express my warmest thanks. Any shortcomings or faults in this book are obviously mine alone.

If anyone desires to read in greater detail about the history of Canada's great police force, I would suggest *The Law Marches West*, by Sir Cecil Denny; *The Northwest Mounted Police*, by J. P. Turner; *The Silent Force*, by T. Morris Longstreth, and *The Royal Canadian Mounted Police*, by R. C. Fetherstonhaugh.

RICHARD L. NEUBERGER

ROYAL CANADIAN MOUNTED POLICE

1

Canada—The Land the Mounties Patrol

COME WITH ME TO THE LAND WHICH PEOPLE CALL CANADA.

Everybody has heard of this vast land. Yet few of us know Canada except as a name, a strange name that has come down through the centuries from the word of the Huron Indians meaning "settlement." This word, *Kanata,* was pronounced "Canada" by the first white men who heard it, and so it has remained.

Canada covers a greater area than the United States. It is nearly as large as the whole continent of Europe. Only Russia and China among the nations of our planet exceed Canada in size.

But Canada is more than mere size. Her beauty and grandeur stir wonder in all who see this good neighbor of the United States. Few realms on earth are cloaked so generously with forests and mountains and rivers and lakes.

I learned something about these mountains, a few years back, when I was riding on a famous Canadian train, the Continental Limited. At one point the train stopped so that we could see a snowy mountain which towered right beside the tracks.

"Gee, Daddy," said a little boy from Chicago, "will we climb that mountain while we're in Jasper Park?"

The boy's father only smiled, but the train conductor had overheard. He said: "Sonny, no one has climbed Mount Robson for ten years. Some of the greatest Mount Everest climbers failed to get to the top of that mountain or to the tops of many other mountains very near here."

We were silent as the Continental Limited started again. All around one of Canada's busy train tracks were mountains as hard to climb as the terrible Himalayas!

Consider just one river of Canada. This river symbolizes how little we know of the country that shares with the United States the longest international border in the world without forts or guns.

The river is the Mackenzie, which flows farther than Ol' Man River himself, the Mississippi. It carries more water down to the sea than the fabled Nile of Egypt. The Mackenzie measures 2,635 miles in length, from its source as a bubbling creek in the Canadian Rockies to the delta of many channels where it unites with the Arctic Ocean.

We think of the mighty Yukon as an Alaskan river. Yet the Yukon is cradled in a chain of deep blue lakes on the soil of Canada.

Even the Columbia, the historic river of our own states of Oregon and Washington, the river that foams through Bonneville and Grand Coulee Dams—even the Columbia has its birthplace among the Canadian glaciers. Rugged mountains form the gigantic bedposts from which these frozen fields of ice are hung like a huge hammock.

Although Canada is larger in area than the United States, it has only about ten per cent of our population. But Canada today is growing more rapidly than any other nation in the world. It has accepted thousands of immigrants who have crossed the oceans to seek a new start in life.

Yet in Canada there still are primitive uplands of the kind our pioneer forefathers saw long ago. Through these uplands roam grizzlies, bighorn sheep, and moose with lordly antlers. I have camped in lonely parts of British Columbia where there were so many moose that we had to be careful they did not step on us during the night!

Wildlife that has almost disappeared from the United States continues to live, free of cages and padlocks, in the boundless outdoors of Canada. The savage brown bears of the western seacoast are among the biggest of meat-eating creatures. Caribou and reindeer furnish food for isolated tribes of Indians and Eskimos.

From an airplane I have watched musk oxen forming a circle on the Canadian barren lands, where only moss grows. Into this square the big animals herded the baby musk oxen. Then the adult musk oxen lowered their heads in a shaggy stockade. It would be a foolish wolf pack, indeed, which would brave that wall of sharp horns and flying hooves!

Once, in a thick clump of pine trees on the Nechako

River in British Columbia, I lay patiently with two young sons of a homesteader. We were near the family's garbage dump. Soon we saw one bear, then two, finally three! As we watched, they pawed the garbage hungrily. Each one of them must have weighed half a ton.

"Our father never lets us go far from the cabin without him," said one of the boys. "And he always takes his gun."

I looked again at the huge bears. Then I replied, "Your

father has good judgment. Be sure you never stop listening to what he says!"

The Canadian solitudes are not only danger-filled, but mysterious, too. I have been aboard a Diesel tug, cruising over cold lakes that were like immense inland seas. It was easy to be out of sight of shore.

Great Bear Lake dwarfs some of the Great Lakes. Ice dots Great Bear Lake all the time except right at midsummer. It is churned by angry storms which rival those of the Atlantic.

On the edge of Great Bear Lake is the pitchblende mine from which comes ore for the atomic bomb. All the barges that haul the ore in the few ice-free months are named *Radium*. There is a reason for this: the mine is also the source of the burning element which can destroy some of the most dreaded diseases.

Look again at the broad map of Canada. Perhaps you can locate Mount Logan, which is a full mile higher than the loftiest mountain in the United States or the highest Alp of Switzerland.

Japanese and Swiss guides traveled thousands of miles to make the first ascent of Mount Alberta, near Banff and Jasper Parks.

"Why have you come?" they were asked. "Are there no great mountains in your own countries?"

"There are," answered the visitors, "but none so inspiring to us as these grand mountains of Canada!"

Thus we are often brought to realize how scant has

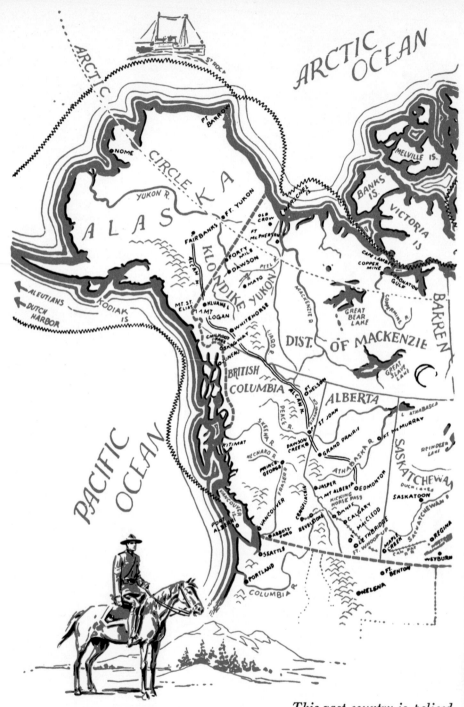

This vast country is policed

by the Canadian Mounties.

been our knowledge of Canada, the land which is the friendliest neighbor and ally of our own nation.

Each time we peer at a map or atlas we discover some startling new fact about Canada. We are proud of the 1,519-mile Alaska Highway, threading through groves of spruce to Fairbanks. Is it a surprise to learn that 1,220 miles of this marvelous road lie within the boundaries of Canada?

We like to think of those courageous explorers, Lewis and Clark, as the first of all white men to span the continent on which we live. Yet, here again, we must gaze northward. Twelve full years before Lewis and Clark saw the Pacific's surf, a man in tattered moosehide came to the end of a long journey at a bay of salt water on the western seacoast. He scribbled in his notebook that he stood at Latitude 52° 20' 48" N. There he painted this story with red clay on a rock:

> Alexander Mackenzie, from Canada, by land, July 22, 1793.

Canada is a country where people love to tell of these great deeds of the past. To me, the tales of Canada are particularly colorful and romantic because they frequently come in two languages, English and French. Ever since the era of the daring *voyageurs* from France, who paddled through the rapids of the hurtling rivers, both languages have appeared on Canadian paper money and postage stamps. The two tongues still are spoken in the spired buildings of Parliament, where Canada's laws are made.

When the lamplights are low in paneled dining halls in the capital city of Ottawa, men fill their coffee cups and puff contentedly on fat cigars. Then it is that the gallant legends are whispered. Somebody urges, "Tell us a story, a great story!"

More likely than not, it may be the same story that is being told at some lonely bivouac in the far-off forests of the Yukon, where the campfire waves and tosses like a ballet dancer. As the tale unfolds, the Northern Lights seem to twist across the sky overhead with special brilliance.

And the thrilling stories never end. There are the stories of the French in their sleek canoes and of the Scotsmen who brought the first trade goods of the Hudson's Bay Company into the trackless North. There are tales of the soldiers who fought each other bloodily at Quebec, and of the Polar mariners who disappeared with the vessels *Erebus* and *Terror* off Canada's tundra shores.

But when the banquet tables have been cleared in Ottawa, and when the aurora borealis flickers at its wildest in the Yukon night, the tales turn to a subject which makes the pulse of every Canadian beat faster with pride.

These are the most stirring tales of all. They kindle the flame of heroism and they make people think of the knights of old. These are the tales of the wilderness police, of the men in scarlet jackets who were banded together in

1873 to bring the Queen's law to the wide open spaces of the West.

This force is known today as the Royal Canadian Mounted Police. Its long arm extends from the busy cities near the American border to the North Magnetic Pole, from Newfoundland's codfish banks to the runs of Tyee salmon which British Columbia shares with Alaska.

The story of the Royal Mounted is the story of Canada as a nation. It also is the story of troopers with a bold motto that has not changed for almost eighty years. This motto is engraved in French on the official badge of the Mounted Police as *Maintiens le Droit*. Its English meaning all men can understand:

"Uphold the Right."

2

"The Finest Police Force in the World!"

I FIRST REALLY GOT TO KNOW THE MOUNTIES WHEN I shipped out to the Yukon Territory on the steamer *Aleutian* in 1942 as aide-de-camp to General James A. O'Connor of the United States Army Engineers.

General O'Connor was assigned to build the first land route in history to Alaska. The Japanese invasion of Kiska and Attu Islands had made such a life-line necessary. Who knew when the sea lanes might be cut?

In the Vancouver Hotel, as our regiment had a last round of roast-beef dinners, we talked to a detective who was dressed in a neat blue business suit and a felt hat. He wanted to learn when the outfit would shove off. These were some of the other questions he asked:

"Are you all ready to sail?"

"Has the date of sailing been kept a secret?"

"Will the equipment for constructing a military highway to Alaska go with you on this ship or follow later on?"

"Who is in charge of security and protection for safeguarding the second ship's departure?"

The detective wrote down our answers in a little leather notebook. He also asked us our full names and Army serial numbers. I thought that his pleasant round face and twinkling brown eyes made him look considerably more like my old scoutmaster of Troop 69 than like a detective.

Three weeks later, 1,250 rugged wilderness miles north of Vancouver, General O'Connor shook hands with a rangy young man in a buffalo-hide greatcoat. Through the lapels of the coat could be seen a scarlet tunic on which the brass initials "R. C. M. P." caught the last faint gleam of Arctic sunlight. The uniform was completed by a hat of muskrat pelts, a carbine strapped over his shoulder, gold-striped breeches on his legs, and snuggly moccasins with colored beads on his feet.

"Sergeant Allen at your service, sir," the stalwart young man told the General.

As he stood beneath the flag at the lonely log outpost along the headwaters of the Yukon River, he satisfied all our boyhood memories of the great tales which have come out of the North Country.

Between the homespun detective in Vancouver and the brilliantly-clad Constable at Caribou Crossing, no one would sense a connection at first. How different their duties seemed to be! Yet both of them came to our Army outfit with the credentials of the same organization—the Royal Canadian Mounted Police.

More than three-quarters of a century after they were officially founded, the Mounties are still the most extraordinary police force in the world. No other law-enforcement agency in any land has duties so widely varied.

The authority of the Royal Mounted stretches from the

busy Canadian industrial cities within sight of Detroit to the ice-sheathed islands guarding the North Pole.

The payroll of the Royal Canadian Mounted Police includes plain-clothes men in Toronto and storm-tossed sailors off the capes of Labrador. Among its members are fingerprint experts in Regina and troopers in parkas and fur trousers who patrol the shores of Hudson Bay by dog sled.

Where these men are in charge, the crime rate is the lowest on the North American continent. Criminals realize that eventually they will be captured. Consider the amazing fact that during one recent year there were only eight murders in the province of Manitoba, where the Mounties enforce practically all the laws. But the Maryland city of Baltimore, with a mere twenty per cent more people than Manitoba, had a hundred murders in the same year!

Although a Mountie Constable begins at the salary of only $5.65 a day and sometimes must serve a dozen years before becoming a Corporal, a long waiting list often seeks admission to the force. Acceptances are comparatively few because the Royal Mounted never send two men to do one man's job.

The Mounties remember the frontier Sergeant who rode alone to Sitting Bull's camp. While the Sioux chief held a rifle at his heart, the Sergeant demanded the surrender of three warriors suspected of breaking the law. He galloped off with the Indians in tow.

"If we had sent a lot of men, there might have been bloodshed," said this brave Sergeant. "But just one Mounted Policeman riding into that big Indian camp sort of took Sitting Bull by surprise. He was off balance and he handed over the braves without a complaint."

The Mounties still get along in this way. They have a total enlistment of 4,855 men. This is fewer than serve in the police department of Los Angeles. It also is a smaller number than the strength of the Philadelphia City Police. Yet the Mounties perform for Canada the same duties which in the United States require the F.B.I., the Coast Guard, Secret Service, Border Patrol and many separate State Police organizations.

Thrift in manpower is a standard policy of the Mounted. They take pride in the story of 400 unruly Cree Indians who were being escorted to Canada for wintering on a new reservation. This was about 1880, in the era when the frontier still was being settled. A column of U. S. Cavalry guarded the tribe. At the international boundary near Medicine Hat, they were met by a Royal Mounted Corporal and two Constables. The Cree warriors smiled on seeing the Mounties, whom they often called "pony soldiers."

"Where's your escort for these Indians?" asked the American commanding officer.

"We're here, Colonel," answered the Mountie Corporal.

"Yes, yes, I see. But where's your regiment?"

"We're here," the Corporal said again.

The Sergeant demanded the surrender of the three warriors.

"Yes, I know. But aren't there any more of you?"

"Oh, yes, sir, Colonel," said the Corporal. "There's a fourth chap, but he's back up in the hills frying a mess of trout for our breakfast."

As we of the Army Engineers spread out through the Yukon and Northwest Territories to build a supply line to Alaska, we found a handful of Mounties policing a region as big as all outdoors. Their exploits made even rugged and toughened American soldiers marvel.

We would come down in a small Norseman plane on the only landing strip in a rolling wilderness the size of the state of Indiana. We would be greeted by a couple of Mounties, and we would learn that they were the law in that whole vast area.

But they were more than the law. They were also doctors, nurses, social workers, tax collectors, game wardens, judges, and explorers. They even were map-makers and parsons at times, too.

People came to the Royal Mounted with every possible problem. A pack of timber wolves might be raiding a caribou herd on which an Indian tribe depended for food and clothing. A fire had burned a backwoods school in the night. Who would organize traders and trappers and prospectors to cut logs for a new schoolhouse? These tasks fell to the Mounties.

"I've helped deliver babies and I've also gone in search of Eskimos who were suspected of abandoning their old men and old women to the terrible cold," said a Mountie with a brushlike mustache that reminded us of pictures of Rudyard Kipling.

At lonely settlements on the Yukon and Mackenzie Rivers we always saw four buildings. These were a Hudson's Bay Company post, a Church of England mission, a Catholic church or mission, and a Royal Canadian Mounted Police barracks.

The Canadian government in distant Ottawa would be represented only by the broad-shouldered Sergeant. He cut a splendid figure with his peaked summer Stetson hat, gold chevrons, glistening collar badges and heavy service revolver at the end of a corded white lanyard. The lanyard was hooked to the butt of the gun, so the Sergeant would not lose his weapon in a fall or scuffle.

We discovered that the Sergeant held a kind of police court, where wrongdoers in lesser crimes were judged. He brought medicines and serums to natives when they were sick. He collected taxes and customs duties on furs. He also carried mail, counted big game such as reindeer and musk oxen, and he occasionally snowshoed along trap lines.

The Mountie Sergeant was a crack shot. He put to shame even the sharpshooters in our Army regiment. A tin can on a stump was an easy target for him. At a shorter distance, he could shoot a hole squarely through the "A" on the Ace of Spades, from a deck of cards.

We listened intently around a stove made out of a rusty

oil drum, as the Sergeant told us how he had captured the slayers of an Indian trapper. It sounded simple when you knew the trick. He just waited at a post down the river for white men who might turn in skins cured in native fashion.

Before the slayers knew what was up, they saw the familiar uniform. Handcuffs were clamped on their wrists, and they were led away to be tried for their crime.

But in spite of such dramatic arrests as this, to be a Mountie is to be more than an ordinary policeman. Especially in the immense expanses of the North, the Mountie does not limit himself to tracking down scoundrels. He also looks after the welfare of the good people.

On Treaty Day it is the Mountie who counts out five new crisp dollar bills for each Indian man, woman, and child. This keeps a pledge made by the government in a treaty many years ago. It was a pledge to be honored for "as long as the grass shall grow." The Mountie takes off his everyday jacket of cocoa-brown color and puts on his scarlet tunic. Then the tribes know a great occasion is at hand.

Canada has a program for children called Family Allowances. These allowances go to *all* families, regardless of income or color. For each child under 6 years of age, a mother receives $5 every month. Between the ages of 6 and 10, the sum increases to $6. A child from 10 years old to 13 merits $7. From the ages of 13 to 16, the monthly amount goes up to $8. The money is paid directly to the mother, but it is supposed to be spent only for the benefit of the children.

In the solitudes which lie far beyond the big cities of Canada, the Mounties manage this program. They are the persons most closely acquainted with the native families. Furthermore, they realize what is best for these simple people.

On visits to the North since the war, I have watched Mounties helping native mothers do their ordering. This has been made possible by the Family Allowances from the government. Because the money is really for the children, the Mounties suggest the buying of such things as pablum, powdered eggs, cream of wheat and canned fruit juices.

"Eskimo children require foods which often are lacking in the native diet, so careful attention must be given to foods bought with Family Allowances money," said Constable Van Norman. As a member of the Pond Inlet detachment of the Mounted Police, he lives 350 miles north of the Arctic Circle. With one other Constable, he patrols an area about the size of the state of New York.

Once a Chipewyan Indian mother reached for a big tempting box of chocolate candy. She was using the credits provided by the government at the Hudson's Bay post for her children. A stalwart Mountie constable with a boyish grin gently put the candy back in its place.

"No, my friend," said he. "I think this might be better

for the little ones." And the Mountie pointed to shelves of canned pineapple and condensed milk.

In many parts of the North, the highest ambition of an Eskimo is to be a Special Constable for the Mounties. A Special Constable helps train Huskies and malemutes to be good sled dogs. He frequently acts as interpreter and he even learns to operate the radio which keeps in touch with far-off headquarters.

When the Mountie faces a perilous mission, the Special Constable often shares his dangers. They become a team. White man and Eskimo take turns at breaking trail, making campfires, and feeding the dogs. They depend completely upon one another.

If a man crumbles through the ice of a creek, his companion must have a roaring blaze crackling in a few moments or the drenched man could freeze to death. The weather can be so cold that several minutes without heavy fur mittens may cause permanent damage to a hand or fingers.

But not every post has Special Constables. Sometimes a Mountie must brave the Arctic all alone. This is why many members of the force diligently study native tongues.

In an isolated detachment beside a tributary of the Yukon River, I heard a young Mountie mumbling under his breath. I was worried. Had the loneliness made him "stir crazy"?

Perhaps he read my thoughts. "No, I'm not wacky," he said. "I'm sound of mind and body. I'm just repeating my lessons in the Nahani Indian language to myself. I get lessons twice a week from the teacher at the native school."

Not so long ago a trooper of the Mounted named Cliff De Lisle traveled 1,500 miles by sled to arrest an Eskimo woman, Mitkayout, who was reported to have shot her brother-in-law. This is a longer distance than from New York City to Omaha, Nebraska, but the Mountie had no assistance on the whole journey.

In a raging blizzard De Lisle and his twelve dogs ran out of food. Only a chance shot at a wandering polar bear kept them from starving to death. The Huskies already had tried to eat the leather harness with which they pulled the sled. But now man and dogs could live off bear meat for many days.

In addition to arranging for Mitkayout to come to trial, De Lisle talked with 750 different Eskimos. He also investigated six accidental deaths. In one of these a young tribesman had frozen to death after a hungry bear drove him from his igloo. During his journey the Mountie recorded a total of 104 births and marriages among the people of the white solitudes.

When he finally caught up with Mitkayout, De Lisle was right at the North Magnetic Pole, the area to which a myriad of compasses point. He was farther north than many famous explorers had gone. Yet this solitary journey, so daring to the average man in his armchair by the

TV set, was merely routine to the Mountie in the Northwest Territories.

Dangerous missions, such as that of Constable De Lisle, explain why only single men may enlist in the Royal Mounted. Nor can they marry until they have served at least five years on the force. On top of this, a Mountie must have the approval of his commanding officer before he can take a bride at any time.

Younger members of the Mounted often are chosen for duty which involves great perils. It is better if these men do not have wives and children to worry about.

Another difference separates the Royal Canadian Mounted Police from the usual police force. The Mounties patrol all through one of the world's largest countries. Their jurisdiction is from coast to coast. Most police organizations are limited to a relatively small area, like a city or one state.

In an emergency a Mountie may have to be transferred from one shore of this wide continent to the opposite shore. A lean Constable with heavy eyebrows said to me at Fort McMurray on the great Athabaska River:

"Three weeks ago I was stationed in downtown Winnipeg. Now, here I am in the wilderness. At night I hear the cry of the loon instead of the rumble of trolley cars!"

A single man has more "mobility" than a man who is married. This means his assignment can be changed hurriedly. Elaborate living quarters are not necessary for him. He can live in a tent or a hut or aboard a tossing 70-foot motorboat—and frequently does.

When I was in the North with the American soldiers building the Alaska Highway, I ran into many examples of the faith which the Canadian people have in their police force. They do not expect Mounties just to arrest criminals. They also expect them to "uphold the right," as promised by the motto on their buttons.

I remember a gnarled and grizzled prospector at Whitehorse who told me of an incident he had seen in the gold-rush days.

A drunken man was thrown out of a saloon and into the cold gooey mud of the frontier street. A Mountie saw this happen. He stood in the doorway of the saloon and called for the bartender to come out. Something in the Mountie's tone of voice made the bartender obey quickly. The Mountie was swinging his swagger stick with impatience.

When the bartender came through the swinging doors, the Mountie said to him:

"I want you to pick up this man and get him a hotel room. Let him stay in the hotel until he sleeps off his drunk. After that, buy him a suit of clothes to replace the one ruined by all this mud. The man was welcome in your saloon as long as his pockets were full of gold dust. You didn't throw him out until he was broke. I'm holding you responsible for his condition."

And my friend, the old prospector, added, "That's why we trust the Mounties. A regular policeman might have

arrested the poor drunken man. But not that Mountie. He knew what had been going on. He made the greedy bartender dance to his tune."

All of us in the Northwest Service Command of the United States Army came to have new respect for Canada's famous wilderness police. If we were stumped by a hard problem, somebody generally suggested, "Let's see the Mounties. Maybe they'll have the answer."

Only the Royal Mounted had any idea of the river

gullies and caribou trails when we had to lay an oil pipe-
line through the unmapped mountains between the Yukon
and Mackenzie watersheds.

It was the Mounties who told us how to survive in the
lowest temperatures on the North American continent.
They said that men trapped in a blizzard on the highway
should roll up in their eider-down sleeping bags, instead of
trying to walk to camp. The Mounties explained that
three separate pairs of thin socks were warmer than one
pair of heavy socks. This was because the air space between the layers was an insulation against the cold. For
the same reason they told us to wear light mittens under
our thick fur gauntlets.

Inspector Cronkhite at Whitehorse sadly shook his head
when he saw our soldiers wearing leather logging boots.
"They'll pinch the feet and cut off circulation," said he.
"When it gets below zero, you're going to need loose-
fitting galoshes or moccasins and *mukluks* made of animal
skins."

Some of our quartermasters disputed the Mountie officer. They said he didn't know what he was talking about.
But after a few jeep drivers had been treated at the base
hospital for frostbitten toes, the quartermasters confessed
that Inspector Cronkhite knew exactly what he was talking about!

Yet I recall one occasion when the Mounties did not
follow their own advice to keep snugly dressed. This was
when we dedicated the Alaska Highway in the outlying

ramparts of the St. Elias Mountains, loftiest range in Canada. We were not too far from Mount Lucania, 17,150 feet in elevation. Even higher summits towered beyond.

In the crude wooden barracks that night, a picked column of Mounties put spit and polish on their equipment. They were from detachments in the lonely Yukon Territory, detachments with wonderful names—Dawson, Dalton Post, Old Crow, Whitehorse.

A man could see his face reflected in one of the wide Sam Brown belts worn by the Mounties. Their buttons were shined until they glistened like jewels. From a dozen feet away, one might make out the stirring motto: *Maintiens le Droit.*

What an occasion that was! We ate cutlets from mountain sheep which had been shot high in the crags by ski troops. There was broiled Arctic grayling, caught in the icy depths of Kluane Lake. The frame building of pine lumber shook to the winds sweeping down off the glaciers, which twisted like white dragons through the mountains.

Canadian cabinet ministers rolled up in their sleeping bags of double thickness beside the Alaskan Delegate to the Congress of the United States. The Mounties were especially excited because the Army of Canada was to be represented by General George R. Pearkes, who once had been a Mountie himself.

"Yes," said General Pearkes. "I was a Corporal in the Mounted and I patrolled out of Dalton Post by dog sled in winter and on a big roan-colored stallion in summer. Now these Mounties will patrol the Alaska Highway in sedans. Times have changed, indeed!"

A soldier with an accordion played the rollicking folk song *Vive La Compagnie*. The booming voices of the Mounties joined in companionship with those of their American friends:

> *Let every good fellow now fill up his glass,*
> > *Vive la compagnie.*
> *And drink to the health of our glorious class,*
> > *Vive la compagnie.*
> *Vive la, vive la, vive l'amour,*
> > *Vive l'amour, vive l'amour, vive la compagnie . . .*

The next morning at Soldiers' Summit a ribbon of red, white, and blue fluttered across the road. Flags of the United States and Great Britain waved side by side from spruce trees which had been stripped of their branches.

The temperature was 24° below zero. Who could stand such weather without coats? The Mounties could! They huddled together for a moment and voted to take off their greatcoats of shaggy buffalo hide. The scarlet tunic was the symbol of the Royal Mounted and of Canada. On this historic day the spectacular red jacket had to be uncovered. It must be seen. Time enough later to worry about frostbite! Doctor Silverman, the Army surgeon, could take care of that.

As the Mounties stood there at attention in the cold November snows, their vivid uniforms of crimson and gold made us think of the poet's phrase about "the thin red line of heroes." This thin red line had made the wild and desolate Yukon one of the most law-abiding regions on earth.

General O'Conner looked at the Mounties when the ribbon was about to be cut. The motor of the first truck was warming up, ready to start for Fairbanks. The General remembered that the Royal Mounted had led nearly all white people into much of Canada's vast wilderness. He thought of Inspector Moodie and his pioneering Constables, who had blazed some of the route of the Alaska Highway.

"There stand men who represent the finest police force in the world!" said the American General, pointing to the column of Mounties.

Everyone at Soldiers' Summit agreed with General O'Connor. And many of us wondered how the Mounties had come to be this way. Where did they get their beginning? What brought about the founding of the scarlet police?

3

To Uphold the Right

A PLACE WITH THE STRANGE NAME OF FORT WHOOP-UP
started it all.

It was an evil-looking stockade of logs, and it stood on
the high plains where the Belly and St. Mary Rivers
flow together. Today this is near the site of the prosper-
ous city of Lethbridge, Alberta.

Cannon guarded the walls of Fort Whoop-Up. The
logs were polka-dotted with loopholes through which
rifles could be fired. A small opening had been cut in the
thick oaken gate. Through this opening passed the liquid
which set the prairies on fire—whisky.

Fort Whoop-Up was run by whisky traders. They gave
an Indian a pint of whisky for each buffalo robe. The
robes were worth five dollars apiece. The whisky was
merely flavored alcohol. It cost virtually nothing and it
seared a man's insides. Yet one post like Fort Whoop-Up
might collect 9,000 buffalo hides during a single summer.

The whisky robbed the savage Plains Indians of all
reason. They burned farmhouses and murdered settlers.
Ranchers were found scalped, with barbed arrows in their
backs. White women were dragged off naked, to be the

slaves and mates of Indian warriors. Children disappeared. The torture stake was put to horrible use.

"My people—they have been turned to beasts by the fire water," said a chief of the Piegans.

In their hearts, the Indians realized they were being cheated and ruined. If they found a whisky wagon alone on the plains, they often killed the drivers on sight or took them prisoners, which was worse.

But the Indians still were racked by the fiendish desire for liquor. They would offer a fine pony for a quart of foul-smelling rum. It was an urge they could not control.

One night in the wooded Cypress Hills, traders as well as Assiniboine Indians howled and yelled in a wild orgy of drinking. Rot-gut whisky flowed like water. The traders were brutal men. One of them had written to a pal in the United States:

> *Dear Friend,*
> *My partner Will Geary got to putting on airs. I shot him and he is dead. The potatoes is looking well.*
> *Yours,*
> SNOOKUM JIM.

Snookum Jim was the kind of person who reveled with the drunken Assiniboines. By midnight the camp was a seething mass of men and women who had lost all restraint. They ripped off each other's clothes and shouted at the glittering moon. Fist fights took place continually.

In this violent setting, anything could happen. It soon did. A bitter quarrel broke out over ownership of several horses. The difference between the traders and the Indians was that the traders were well-armed with guns. They fired volley after volley into the Indian side of the camp. More than thirty Assiniboines were murdered. The dead included women and little babies.

Homesteaders on the plains were terrified. They feared the Indians would exact a grim revenge for this shocking deed. Every white family barred doors and gates and huddled in terror at night. Already, conditions were so bad that no settler dared to raise livestock. Indians would steal the cattle and horses after sundown.

A half-breed deliberately cut the arm tendons of an Indian woman at the village of Edmonton, making her a cripple. The same man killed another woman in a brawl started by whisky. Yet he went free, to carry on his cruelties. No law punished him for these crimes, for no law existed in the vast reaches of the Canadian West.

Fort Whoop-Up poured liquor over the prairie. A harvest was reaped in death, fire, and torture.

But on July 1, 1867, confederation had taken place among the lonely and isolated provinces of Canada. A Dominion was formed, binding together the separate sections of this vast land. A legal government sat at last in Ottawa. It could do something. It had to do something. The settlers held indignation meetings.

"Has our country deserted us?" cried one of these

angry men. "Will it not protect our families and our property? Have we been abandoned? Must we continue to be pillaged and looted?"

Messengers rode to the capital with these complaints. In May of 1873 Sir John A. Macdonald, Prime Minister of the new nation, asked Parliament for permission to form a force of "Mounted Rifles."

That night the Prime Minister and his counselors met in conference. "Sir John," said a member of the House of Commons, "I fear that a force known as 'the Mounted

Rifles' will make our American friends think an army is on its way to the Canadian West. They will be alarmed. We must emphasize the civilian character of our agency."

"Then it should have a different name," agreed the Prime Minister. "What shall that name be?"

For a few moments there was silence in the paneled room. One or two men toyed with pens. Several studied the maps on the wall. The Prime Minister was the first to break the stillness.

"I believe I know the name for our organization," he said.

All the others listened respectfully.

The Prime Minister next spoke the words which one day would stand for law and order not only in the Canadian wilderness but throughout the world.

"This force we are forming," he suggested, "should be called 'Northwest Mounted Police'."

The others nodded their heads in assent, as the Prime Minister continued. "We need picked men," said he. "They must be men who can make friends with the Indians. They must deal firmly with the whisky traders and other outlaws. They will be only 300 in number, so each man must be able to give a good account of himself."

"And they must wear red coats," chimed in Colonel Patrick Robertson-Ross, the Adjutant-General of Canada.

"And why, pray tell?" asked a member of Parliament.

"Because the uniform of the Northwest Mounted Police must be a symbol—a symbol of right and justice," replied Colonel Robertson-Ross. "I have been in the West. I know that the Indians have faith in symbols. Red, to them, is the color of the Queen. They have heard that the regiments of the Great White Mother wear red. Our police force, too, must wear red."

"The Colonel has a point," said Prime Minister Macdonald. "Our 300 policemen must uphold the law in a land where thousands and thousands of Indians live. Perhaps a symbol will help them. The tunic shall be red."

And now the call went forth.

Canada needed her strongest sons. They had to be men of stout heart and broad shoulders. They had to be between the ages of eighteen and forty. They had to read and write either English or French. And they had to be ready for any hardship. Love of country was more important than desire for money. No Mountie would get rich. The lowest-ranking Constable would be paid only seventy-five cents a day!

The call was answered. From everywhere they came— lumberjacks and clerks, chefs and college students, farmers and day laborers. Some sought adventure. Some wanted to be free of a shady past. A few hoped to escape from nagging wives. Several had an ambition to homestead beyond the Rockies. Some just dreamed romantically of wearing a scarlet jacket and riding into the unknown West on a great horse that stood fifteen and a half hands high.

Of course, the laggards had to be weeded out. A man

who fell off his horse too many times was unsuited for the Mounted Police. Quarrelsome recruits were sent home. There would be enough fighting with whisky traders and Indian hostiles. The Mounties could have no trouble-makers in their own ranks.

One or two of the original Mounties had served some jail time themselves. The officers worried about these men. Could they be trusted in an organization which was to "uphold the right"? Yet every person was entitled to a chance. Perhaps these men had reformed. After all, history was full of examples of people who had risen to prominence after a first mistake.

"We are going into a hard land," said the commander of the Mounties, Commissioner George A. French. "We may need some hard characters on our side."

The recruits were to travel westward from Camp Dufferin, in the province of Manitoba. To reach Dufferin in comfort, the Mounties had to take off their uniforms and enter the United States. They journeyed on the new Northern Pacific Railroad to Fargo, North Dakota, where the tracks ended. Dufferin was a short horseback jaunt directly north of Fargo.

In July of 1874 the Mounties, 300 strong, set out to save the Canadian West from its legacy of death and horror.

Ride with them as they go, these troopers who are the first of a long line of recruits in the wilderness police. They wear tight red jackets, blue breeches with yellow

The Mounties, 300 strong, set out for the Canadian West.

stripes, and high black boots. A little flat pillbox cap, shaped like a tambourine, surmounts their heads. In the knapsacks are gleaming white helmets with brass spikes, for fancy dress and parades. As they stream out of Dufferin, the mellow notes of a bugle call float over the prairie.

Pierre from Quebec, who cannot speak English, rides beside Thomas from Toronto, who cannot speak French. The son of an English duke jogs stirrup to stirrup with the son of a bricklayer. A tall man brought up on an English country estate listens to the broken dialect of a stocky man who grew up in distant Bohemia.

Robust Americans, enlisted on the sly as the Northern Pacific train stopped in St. Paul, swap racy tales with trappers hailed from the Manitoba muskeg bogs. The bearded Assistant Commissioner, James F. Macleod, born in Scotland, rides along in a reverie of his own thoughts. Already he knows it will be his special assignment to put Fort Whoop-Up out of business and end the evil whisky trade.

A messenger gallops up excitedly when they are only a few miles out of Dufferin. He has a last important letter for one of the troopers. The man opens it and gives a great shout.

"Listen to this, comrades," he reads. "I have kept a book too long from the Winnipeg library. For this I owe three cents a day. I shall be arrested unless I pay the fine."

A roar of laughter comes from the others who have

heard. The incident seems to have relaxed the tension. The officers are grateful. Dufferin has barely disappeared behind the horizon before the difficulties of the trek begin to be evident.

Water holes are few and far between. The horses gasp and choke in the midsummer prairie heat of 100 degrees. Troopers are miserably uncomfortable in their uniforms which fit like glue. When a creek is reached, the horses must drink first. The water is a muddy gumbo by the time the men can quench their thirst.

Dysentery breaks out. The Constables retch in their saddles and sway weakly, trying to hold on to the reins of the horses. Grasshoppers settle on the carts and wagons in a dark cloud, devouring quantities of the precious food supplies. Prairie cholera attacks some of the men who drank too greedily of alkali water. They lose weight rapidly. All food sickens them.

The short grass of the plains has not been nourishing enough to sustain stable-fed horses. They can no longer carry their riders. Many of the Mounties must get off and walk. The proud jackets of scarlet are dirty and torn. Boots shred to pieces from mile after mile of weary trudging. A man who has worn out two pairs now has his feet wrapped in blankets and rags.

"I thought this was going to be peaches and cream," grumbles a trooper whose mount has given out.

"Nobody made you come along," replies another.

Commissioner French watches his column carefully. Will these exhausted policemen be able to subdue whisky traders and inspire respect in Indians? The Commissioner is reassured on a hot, sticky Sunday when the men voluntarily hold a church service. Some sing hymns in English, others in the lilting language their forefathers brought from France.

A sand crane flaps away clumsily as the strains of *Lead, Kindly Light* roll across the prairie. The bird could have been a meal for a few of them but no man reaches for the pistol at his cartridge belt. For a moment they are far in thought from the dusty plains.

And so on the Mounties plod. Often they are hungry. Frequently they are sick. Most of the time they are oppressed by the stifling prairie heat. And always they realize that the inevitable coming of winter will turn this furnace into an aching, frigid ice box.

But are the hardships a total loss? Can no good at all be counted from them? Commissioner French is not without hope. He remarks to the whiskered Macleod: "It is well that the men should have some idea of the obstacles which will be presented by the task ahead of them."

They are the only peace officers in an area of 2,250,000 square miles. Soon they will be 1,000 miles from the nearest Canadian official authority. They will be beyond the reach of mail and telegraph. The government at distant Ottawa is but a memory. They are 300 men on their own.

Some day they may have to answer to the authority of Parliament. But now arrows and war drums and ugly stockades are a more immediate matter.

The odds against the Mounties are at least 10 to one, possibly even 100 to one. How can 300 men patrol so vast an area? Yet never can the Mounties forget the purpose of their mission. Always the motto on their buttons will serve as a reminder of what that mission is:

"Uphold the Right."

4

"Stamix Otokon" Makes Peace with the Indians

BOND, THE WHISKY TRADER, HAD NOT YET HEARD OF THE
coming of the rugged, red-coated Mounties. His wagon
bounced joltingly over the rough ground, but Bond was
happy. This journey in the year 1874 already had brought
him 116 buffalo robes, and the trip was young. The
wagon was heavy with kegs of alcohol, and the Indians
were eager to offer him a buffalo pelt for each fiery pint.

Four of Bond's men drove wagons behind him. They
were armed with Henry rifles. A wandering tribe would
think twice before it fell on such a party and tried to take
the whisky by force. Most of the traders were dead shots.

In his mind, Bond was spending the rich profits which
he felt sure would be his. He thought longingly of the
gambling casinos and plush hotels in Helena, south of the
border.

Life seemed good to Bond, the whisky trader. He had
even built his own stockade. He wasn't going to divide
his money with the Fort Whoop-Up gang.

From out of the dusk came a command:

"Halt, in the name of the Queen!"

Bond, an American, had not remembered that the
British Empire was ruled by a Queen, whose name was

Victoria. But now Bond saw before him a tall man on a prancing horse. The man wore a red jacket with frayed cuffs. On his head was a snow-white helmet. Behind him in the gloom were other men on horseback. Bond knew nothing of the Northwest Mounted Police, but he sensed danger.

One of Bond's men reached for a rifle at his feet.

"I'd put that down if I were you," said the tall man quietly. The trader hesitated, then dropped the gun.

Inspector Crozier lifted a heavy tarpaulin on the wagon driven by Bond. Beneath the canvas he saw casks of whisky, sinister rows of rifles, and heaps of buffalo robes.

"I think we'd better go to Fort Macleod," said the Inspector.

"Where's that?" asked the whisky trader.

"You'll soon find out," replied the Mountie, a man with a thick dark mustache.

At Fort Macleod, first police post in the West, the Constables already were in barracks but the officers still lived in tents. Macleod believed in the best food and quarters for the enlisted men. The Mountie officers came last. He thought this was the way to have high morale in a difficult situation.

The traders were brought before the Assistant Commissioner. He eyed them sternly while Inspector Crozier presented the evidence. Macleod fingered one of the thick robes.

"The Indians need these for tepees and for clothing,"

"Halt, in the name of the Queen!"

he said. "You have taken away their robes and given them nothing except alcohol, which wrecks their health and ruins their sanity."

The traders shifted their feet nervously.

For possessing liquor in Indian country, each of the whisky traders was fined fifty dollars. The head trader, Bond, had to pay a fine of $200 and go to the log jail, because he sold alcohol to an Indian named Three Bulls. The Indian testified against Bond at the brief trial.

The traders cursed angrily as the Mounties opened the casks and let the whisky run out into the snow. The buffalo robes were returned to the Indians.

"Tell your friends this is only the beginning," said Macleod to the traders, who went free after paying their fines.

Prospects suddenly had become gloomy for the whisky runners. They never knew when a scarlet-coated trooper on horseback would confront them along the trail. They would see their profits poured out of the kegs. The robes would be handed back to the Indians, who were shivering in the bitterly-cold prairie winter.

"When I return to the United States I'll wire my Congressman in Washington, D. C.," threatened one wealthy trader, whom Macleod sentenced to jail.

"Give him my respectful regards," answered the leader of the Mounties.

Macleod never learned whether the indignant trader's Congressman eventually protested to the Canadian Foreign Minister in Ottawa. These pioneer Mounties were out of touch with their own government. Since leaving Dufferin and marching toward the sunset, they had received no pay and no mail from home. They were living off the land. The men did not even have enough money to buy pipe tobacco at isolated posts.

Macleod had to ride hundreds of miles across the boundary into Montana, to Fort Benton on the upper Missouri River. There at last he could wire headquarters at Ottawa, asking if his troopers ever were going to be paid their pittance of seventy-five cents a day.

"Bank at Helena will honor your requests," Ottawa replied.

No railroad reached the gay Territorial capital of Montana in those frontier days. Guided by Jerry Potts, who was half-Blackfoot and half-Scotsman, the Macleod party slogged through a blizzard in which the temperature dropped to 60 degrees below zero.

Inspector Cecil Denny was blinded temporarily by the glaring snow. He could not see his hand in front of his face. The Mounties would have frozen to death if Potts had not found a cave below a steep bluff. They could not get a fire going and had to eat their buffalo meat raw. The singing of roistering songs kept them from going to sleep, because they did not know if they ever would awaken in that numbing cold. Their trousers of bison hide were frozen so stiff that they could hardly bend the garments at the knees.

But when at last they reached Helena, they slept in fine beds and ate juicy beefsteaks with fried potatoes and sweet corn. Still more important, they drew $35,000 out of the bank on the credit of the Canadian government. The Constables with empty purses at Fort Macleod now could be paid.

Despite their lack of money, these Constables were stamping out the whisky trade. For more than ten years this trade had thrived. Several thousand American cavalrymen in Montana had not been able to stop it. One reason was that they were forever fighting Indians. They had no time to chase the whisky outlaws.

"If three hundred of us are to do what whole regiments have been unable to accomplish, we must make friends with the Indians," said Macleod.

This was done by being firm but just. On one occasion, several troopers were visiting a tribal camp when an old Indian poked a gun through a hole in a tepee. He fired and his pretty young wife fell dead by the fire. The aged man explained that she had been making eyes at a handsome young Indian, so he seemed to think he had done no wrong in killing her. He looked upon his wife as only another piece of property.

"You have committed a crime," said one of the Constables. "You must stand trial. You have no right to kill."

Friends of the old man crowded angrily around the Mounties. They held guns and bows and arrows. But the chiefs realized the police meant business. If these Mounties were slain, others would surely come. The Indians would have to answer for what had been done.

The aged Indian was taken to Winnipeg, where he heard a judge sentence him to five years in prison for killing his wife. After this, Indians no longer treated their women like cattle.

Assistant Commissioner Macleod had planned to lay siege to Fort Whoop-Up. But the siege was not necessary. The Mounties had squeezed the profit out of the whisky trade. It had become too hazardous. The few shipments which sneaked by the police were more than offset by the countless gallons that the scarlet-jacketed troopers poured onto the ground. Thousands of dollars also were collected by the Mounties in fines.

On the streets of Helena, the traders had bragged to their lady friends about the terrible things they would do to the Northwest Mounted Police. They would fix those Mounties!

But now, under cover of night, the whisky ring abandoned Fort Whoop-Up, the post which had brought so much misery and suffering to the people of the Canadian plains. The stockade had lost its value.

When the Mounties rode to Fort Whoop-Up, they found only a caretaker, who swung open the heavy gates and greeted them cordially. "Come in, gentlemen!" he cried. "The fort is all yours."

Word spread over the prairie that fire water would flow no more among the Indian tribes. Even Indians who most craved it seemed to realize they would be better off. They had been freed from the terrible temptations offered by the whisky traders. The chiefs rejoiced. Never again would liquor turn hundreds of their simple people into bloodthirsty bandits and killers.

The chiefs knew who had accomplished this miracle. It was the man who had led "B," "C," and "F" companies of the Mounted Police into the Cypress Hills. They were generous in their praise of Macleod, whom they called *Stamix Otokon*. This meant "Buffalo Bull's Head" and resulted from the horned bison which appeared on the insignia decorating the Mounties' badges and buttons.

Said Button Chief, a famous warrior of the Bloods, one of the leading tribes of the Blackfoot nation:

"The Great Mother (Queen Victoria) sent *Stamix Otokon* and the police to put an end to the traffic in fire water. I can now sleep safely. Before the arrival of the police, when I laid my head down at night, every sound frightened me. My sleep was broken. Now I can sleep sound and I am not afraid."

With Macleod in the rolling hills along the international border, there were fewer than 175 men. The small size of his force may have been a real factor in Macleod's success.

When the Indians saw the United States Cavalry, they saw a vast number of massed riders on horseback. This roused them to war. An immense horde seemed to be swooping down on the homeland of the Indians. They would oppose it with a huge war party of their own.

Furthermore, land companies and railroads, eager to lay claim to the most fertile valleys, often could bring political pressure on the American troops to drive the Indians from their favorite hunting grounds. Two thousand cavalrymen fought 355 Nez Percés under Chief Joseph.

But the Mounted Police came one at a time or by two's or three's. The Indians admired courage, for they wanted to be stout-hearted themselves. Their respect was stirred when they saw a lone trooper in a crimson jacket facing a hostile tribe.

"The Cree is brother to the brave," a Cree chieftain with outstretched hand said to a Sergeant in the Northwest Mounted, who rode alone into camp in quest of Indian horse thieves.

Perhaps the fear of the unknown that lurked in every Indian was prodded, too. Surely men must have a powerful magic if they could afford to be so few in number as the Mounted Police. Was the magic in the glistening buttons which *Stamix Otokon* and his riders wore on their coats of red? The Indians were obviously in awe of the wilderness police.

To add to Macleod's troubles, Sitting Bull and his Sioux galloped furiously across the border from the United States. A continent was crying out for their blood. They had just massacred General George A. Custer and the 7th Cavalry. Could Macleod's handful of Mounties control the 4,000 most savage Indians in North America?

Sitting Bull never let his warriors fire bullets during the hunt. Ammunition was to be saved for use against white men. Bows and arrows would serve to bring down buffalo and elk. This was the Indian chieftain who now faced a few scattered detachments of the Northwest Mounted Police.

Macleod knew that if he showed either fright or favoritism, he and his whole command might be wiped out as completely as Custer's had been. They could go down beneath a wave of hoofs and spears and flaming arrows.

To *Stamix Otokon* the life of an Indian was as sacred as that of a white man. Every person was entitled to the protection of the law. Indians sensed this and knew he was their friend.

Once Macleod reported to headquarters: "I actually was asked by an American who settled here if we had the same law as on the other side, and if he could shoot any Indian who approached his camp after being warned not to advance. Such a rule is not necessary in dealing with the worst of Indians."

Macleod kept his promises. When the Sioux were told they could graze and hunt in a certain area, they were not ordered to leave those woods and swales a few weeks later. The leader of the Mounties turned his back on greedy white settlers who complained the Indians were getting the best forage or water.

Sitting Bull was content. The conqueror of Custer felt that the Mounted Police had dealt fairly with him. But a band of mischievous young Sioux braves made off with some horses belonging to the herd at Fort Macleod.

This was a serious loss to the Mounties, who had no horses to spare. Inspector Allen headed for the great encampment of Indians to get back the steeds. Sitting Bull saw the speck of red in the distance and met the Mountie in a meadow. It was a day when the fierce chief was in a defiant mood. He glared at the police officer.

Inspector Allen said the force wanted the horses which the Sioux warriors had stolen from the pastures near the fort.

"You cannot ever have these horses again," replied Sitting Bull. "They are part of the Sioux herd now."

"Our brand is on them" said the Inspector. "I shall recognize the brand."

"You will not have the chance," said Sitting Bull.

"I would take your own horse from under you, if it had been stolen from its true owner," retorted the Mountie.

"It is a stolen horse," said Sitting Bull tauntingly.

For a moment red-skinned chieftain and red-coated policeman eyed each other directly. Then, without another word, Inspector Allen leaned out of his saddle and put strong arms under Sitting Bull. He lifted the Indian off the horse he was riding and pulled hard on the animal's bridle.

All of a sudden the most feared Indian in North America was dumped on the ground, and Inspector Allen was riding pell-mell for Fort Macleod, with the checkrein of Sitting Bull's horse clutched in his hand.

The chief's loss of face before his people was a more severe blow to Sitting Bull than the loss of the stolen horse. Yet the Indians responded to this kind of bravery. And, in their hearts, they were aware that the Mountie had done right.

"Here we are treated as men," Sitting Bull admitted to Macleod.

For five years the savage Sioux, the tribe which had wiped out Custer's regiment, stayed on Canadian soil. During that time there was not a single major raid or serious uprising. The 175 troopers of James F. Macleod had convinced the 4,000 braves of Sitting Bull that they should keep the peace.

One of the Sioux fighting men had taken General Custer's watch from his bleeding body on the battlefield of the Little Big Horn in Montana. A Sergeant of the Mounted asked the Indian if he could have the timepiece. The next time a courier rode across the border to Fort Benton, Custer's watch was in his saddlebag. It was to go to the widow of the valiant American General as a gift from the Northwest Mounted Police.

In 1877 all the tribes of the Blackfoot nation made a treaty with the Great White Mother in England, through her greatest servant, *Stamix Otokon*.

The Queen was to have part of the land of the Indians,

so that Canada could become a mighty country. Each chief would get fine clothes, a medal, and a flag. All Indians would be paid five dollars a year apiece, for every year thereafter. The Queen would send teachers to show the Indians how to read the Bible and other books. She also would help the Indians to till and cultivate the soil.

While the treaty was being discussed and signed, fifty Mounties in full crimson kit guarded the council. Proclaimed Eagle Tail, chief of the North Piegans:

"The advice and help I received from the police I shall

never forget as long as the moon brightens the night, as long as water runs, and as long as the grass grows in the spring."

Next spoke Crowfoot, greatest leader of the Blackfeet. "If the police had not come to the country, where would we all be now?" he asked dramatically.

Then the aged Indian went on: "Bad men and whisky were killing us so fast that few indeed would have been left today. The police have protected us, as the feathers of the bird protect it from the frosts of winter. I wish the police all good. I hope that our hearts will increase in goodness from this time forward."

Red Crow, chief of the South Bloods, was more to the point. "I trust *Stamix Otokon* and will leave everything to him," said the chief in his plumed headdress. "Before the police came, the Indian walked bent. Now he walks erect."

Stamix Otokon, the bearded Assistant Commissioner of police, stood before his Indian friends. He was very straight and upright in his splendid uniform. Tall Constables in red and gold glistened at attention on each side of him. In the distance a bugler had sounded a long, stirring call. The echoes faded slowly in the trees.

"If these promises ever were broken, I would be ashamed to look you in the face," Macleod said to the Blackfoot leaders. "But every promise will be solemnly fulfilled, as certainly as the sun shines down upon us from the Heavens."

He paused, and perhaps he thought of the dramatic

chain of events which had brought a boy born in Scotland to that wild and colorful scene. It may be that *Stamix Otokon* brooded about the tragic Nez Percé Indians, who even then were trying to break through a line of American regiments, so they could reach the protection of the Mounted Police on Canadian soil.

Tears filled the blue eyes of the leader of the Mounties, as he said to the chiefs:

"I shall always remember the kind manner in which you have spoken to me."

The chiefs of the Blackfoot nation smiled at Macleod, who was their friend. Then they left the council, carrying in their arms the presents from the Queen. The best present of all was a red coat for each of them.

Ever after, on Treaty Day, all Indians in the vast land of Canada have asked that the money symbolizing the pledge by *Stamix Otokon* be paid in the presence of a trooper of the Mounted Police. They have asked, too, that for the occasion the Mountie wear his tunic of scarlet with its brass badges and buttons.

As it was in the beginning, so it had to be forever and ever.

5

The Mounties Show the Railroad the Way

IN APRIL OF 1885 A STRANGE SCENE OCCURRED IN THE heart of the Selkirk Mountain Range, where snowy peaks tower dizzily above timbered valleys.

Three men in red coats faced more than 500 angry rioters at a log bridge over a rushing stream. Inch by inch, the scarlet-jacketed men yielded ground. But at the bridge they stopped. The mob pressed against them. They were jostled and bumped. One of them was struck by a stone. Yet they did not move.

And the mob went no farther. A bighorn sheep, peering down from the crags on this curious encounter, might have been puzzled. The animal could not have known that, long before in history, a Roman hero named Horatius had held a bridge with two companions against a whole attacking army.

And now Sergeant Fury of the Northwest Mounted Police was doing the same thing in the granite corridor of Eagle Pass.

The rioters were workmen hired to build the new Canadian Pacific Railway. Canada's survival as a nation depended upon the completion of this railway. But the company was in financial difficulties. The crews had not been paid and they were rebellious. Gamblers and liquor dealers, eager to get their hands on the pay envelopes of the workers, were helping to stir up the riot.

The police realized that the men had a real grievance. They had a right to be indignant. But the men, to revenge themselves against the company, wanted to burn tool-houses and rip up sections of track.

"That, my friends, we must prevent," said Sergeant Fury to the small detachment of police at Beaver, so named because of the beaver dams on the nearby mountain rivers.

"And," added the Sergeant, "let's hope we can prevent it without hurting anyone in the process."

Into one of Beaver's noisy saloons strode Fury. He arrested a man who was urging the rioters to loot and burn railroad property. The Sergeant had to force his way back through the swinging doors, with the prisoner in tow. The mob kept pace with him, muttering threats.

At the bridge the Sergeant turned. He drew his revolver from its holster. With the other hand he tightened his cartridge belt. In the dust of the road the Mountie scuffed a line with his boot.

"On that side of the line you stay!" he ordered the mob.

Could a tiny cluster of uniformed men hold the bridge against a horde?

The mob pressed forward again. The rioters moved like a living wood against the Mounties. At last it seemed the police would have to give ground because of the sheer weight of numbers. And still they did not shoot. They knew that news of a killing, even in self-defense, would spread along the entire line of the new railway. It might arouse hatreds and bitterness which would never be ended.

The prisoner made a bolt for freedom. Constable Walters felled him with his fist. Bullets had not flown yet!

Suddenly a new voice joined the clamor.

"Stop!"

Superintendent Sam Steele of the Northwest Mounted stood behind his men. He tottered weakly, but a carbine was clutched in his hand. The commander of police had been flat on his back with typhoid fever when he heard the rising shouts of the mob. He had dragged himself from bed to back up the detachment with his presence.

At the sight of a sick man swaying there defiantly on the bridge, the mob broke. Superintendent Steele had arrived at the strategic moment. The ringleader of the mob went to jail and the railroad went through the mountains.

Canada would never have become the proud and powerful country which we know today if those early Mounties had failed in their difficult and dangerous tasks. The fate of a nation rode with them in the saddle.

The vast seacoast province of British Columbia had agreed to join Canada in 1871, only after receiving a promise from the government that a railroad would be built to Vancouver within ten years. And now the railroad was far behind schedule and British Columbia was getting restless.

Some sentiment demanded union with the United States. Many residents were for cutting loose completely and setting up an independent territory. Who wanted to belong to a country which could not even thrust a wagon rut, much less a railway, through the Rockies and the rugged Selkirks? Indignation ran high in British Columbia.

If the Canadian Pacific soon did not tie British Columbia to the distant prairies with bands of steel, the seacoast province would withdraw. Without an outlet on the Pacific Ocean, Canada could never hope to develop into a world power.

And the completion of the Canadian Pacific depended on a handful of Mounties. Would they be able to control the liquor traffic, to keep out crooked gamblers, to placate warlike Indians, to keep peace between the company and the construction workers?

Superintendent McIllree on the Alberta plains heard that a band of laborers had taken possession of a work train and refused to get off. He boarded the train himself to talk to the men. They told him that a contracting company, hired by the railroad, had promised them their fare back to Quebec, once the line had been built as far as Calgary. The track was in Calgary, but now the contractors were going back on their word.

The Superintendent of the Mounties went to the contractors. "Is this true?" he asked.

One of the head contractors began to stutter and stammer. "Is it true what those workmen said?" repeated Superintendent McIllree.

Finally the contractor reluctantly answered, "Yes."

"I'd give them their fare home if I were you," said the Superintendent sternly.

The next day the workers were bound for Quebec, riding in first-class cars in style.

After the treaty between *Stamix Otokon* and the Blackfoot leaders, most of the Indians let the builders of the railroad proceed in peace. But to a few tribes the coming of the snorting steam locomotive meant the end of the buffalo, the end of their plentiful hunting ranges. Some of these tribes refused to accept the advice of Crowfoot, "to live side by side with our white friends, guided by *Stamix Otokon* and the rest of the police."

Indian resistance to the railroad always meant a touch-and-go situation for the Mounties.

Pie-a-Pot and his band of Crees camped directly across the roadbed laid out by Canadian Pacific surveyors. Then the Indians rode in a wide circle, firing rifles and arrows into the air. The track crews fled in terror. From the Maple Creek post of the Mounted Police, a Sergeant and a Constable galloped to the scene. They found themselves confronted by several hundred Indians, all in an ugly mood.

"You'll have to move your camp," the Sergeant told Pie-a-Pot. "You aren't even in a good site for fuel and water. You're just trying to block the railroad."

Pie-a-Pot looked at the Mountie indifferently. "I stay here," he answered. "This place I like."

The Sergeant pulled out of his tunic pocket a thick watch on a gold chain. "I'll give you just fifteen minutes to move," he said to the Cree chief.

Indians danced around the Mountie. Several fired their guns near his face. One made as if to impale him with a spear. But the Mountie sat quietly in the saddle, looking down at his watch. He never changed expression. In those fifteen minutes, the nerves of the Indians became frayed and tormented. They could understand a foe who came at them shrieking and brandishing weapons. They could not understand this silent man who merely studied a little dial.

"Time's up!" said the Sergeant. He got off his horse and handed the reins to the waiting Constable.

The Mountie trudged into the lodge of Pie-a-Pot and kicked over the main pole. Down onto several surprised squaws collapsed the tepee of sewn buffalo hides. The Sergeant did the same thing in four or five other lodges near that of the chief. Squaws hollered and floundered beneath the heavy animal pelts.

Then the Sergeant strode back to where Pie-a-Pot sat. "Now, be on your way," he ordered.

The Indians hastily packed their baggage and rode off. The Sergeant watched them go with a satisfied smile. "If we had threatened them with our revolvers," he told the young Constable, "honor and pride might have made them fight. Blood could have been shed. But this way, they get off the line of the railroad and no one has been killed or hurt. Old Pie-a-Pot won't bother us again. His own people may make fun of him. I kind of feel sorry for Pie-a-Pot."

This was standard practice with the Northwest Mounted. Whether they were policing Indians, contractors, or construction workers, they tried hard to avoid bloodshed. "Never fire first!" more than one Mountie officer told his subordinates. Trigger-happy recruits soon were turned out of the Mounted Police.

This helped to keep order along the line of the new railroad. But it also called for brave men and some paid with their lives.

When Sergeant Charles Colebrook of the Duck Lake detachment rode to arrest the dangerous Cree outlaw Almighty Voice, the Mountie advanced with one hand raised in the sign of peace. His pistol was in its leather holster. He was not frightened by the bad reputation of Almighty Voice. At short range Almighty Voice shot him through the throat. The Sergeant fell dead.

For nineteen months the police hunted for Almighty Voice. It was a pursuit they would never give up. At last they cornered him in a grove in the Minnichinas Hills, but not until he had shot two other Mounties from ambush.

Duck Lake, in the Saskatchewan uplands, was a bloody place in the annals of the Mounted Police, despite their efforts to prevent violence and outright warfare.

At Duck Lake three men of the force were slain and six painfully wounded in a desperate battle between outnumbered Mounties and the *Metis*. These people were led by Louis Riel, a brilliant but violent man who revolted against the Canadian government.

The *Metis* were a tragic group. They were half-breeds, the sons of white traders and trappers and of Indian mothers. They wanted their own agricultural life on the plains, and they elected Riel to Parliament to speak for them. But the government dealt harshly with the *Metis*. Riel was illegally denied his seat in the House of Commons, and the *Metis* could not get deeds to their homestead acres. This was foolish, for a more kindly policy could have made friends of these half-breeds. Riel would not have been able to stir them to revolt.

But, like the cavalry soldiers in the poem *The Charge of the Light Brigade*, the Mounties could not question why. It simply was "theirs to do or die." They had to follow the commands which came to them from Ottawa over the recently-strung telegraph wires.

And once the *Metis* had rebelled against the government, the Mounties had no choice. Law and order had to be restored or Canada would cease to be a sovereign nation. Its currency would not be honored abroad. Its authority would topple at home. The railroad, needed so desperately to make Canada a country reaching from coast to coast, could never be finished with the land in the grip of rebels.

Outflanked in the deep snow at Duck Lake, the Mounties died in a withering fire. But they kept coming. They fought the *Metis* at Cut Knife Hill, where three more men in red coats died in battle. Frequently they were against superior numbers of five to one. Some of the half-breeds had Gatling guns which fired many bullets at once.

Eventually the rebellion was broken. Although the half-breeds were stubborn fighters, their resources were limited. Riel died on the gallows for treason, a death which made him a martyr to thousands of his followers. If only the Canadian politicians had been willing to safeguard the homesteads and farming land of the *Metis*, the whole rebellion might have been prevented.

And now the railroad was really going through. Trains already whistled all the way across the plains. Mounties patrolled in Kicking Horse Pass, one of the most rugged parts of the great chain of mountains known as the Rockies. Yellowhead Pass, off to the north, was far less steep and narrow. But the government wanted the Canadian Pacific Railroad near the international border, to make sure that the ambitious Americans did not change the location of the boundary!

The railroad was to be an anchor. It was to keep the

border in place. For this reason the track had to be laid in the roughest part of North America yet penetrated by a railway. Oftentimes Mounties found themselves on goat trails where their stirrups hung out over thin blue space. They had to ford glacial streams at points which were perilously near the lips of waterfalls that tumbled in plumes of spray through the clear mountain air.

On November 7, 1885, the last section of track was laid and a stout iron spike was driven in the presence of company officials and Mounties in full uniform. The Canadian Pacific had no money to spare for gold spikes and other frills! A little station named Craigellachie was built to mark the historic point where the railroad had been completed. In Scotland a castle of this name was the meeting place of a clan which had as its battle cry the shout, "Stand Fast!"

And the Mounties had stood fast. They had never wavered. Sir William Van Horne, the determined builder of the Canadian Pacific, had this to say about them:

"Without the splendid assistance of the officers and men of the Northwest Mounted Police, it would have been impossible to accomplish what we did. On no great work within my knowledge, where so many men have been employed, has such perfect order prevailed."

The Mounties, ever loyal to their Indian friends, suggested that the new railroad give a pass to Crowfoot. Had he not persuaded the Blackfeet to let the endless dragon of steel be laid on their lands without bloodshed and

The Canadian Pacific Railroad was really going through.

fighting? The pass was to permit Crowfoot to ride on Canadian Pacific trains for as long as he lived.

The chief was grateful. Through the scarlet-coated police, he sent a reply to Van Horne. This is what Crowfoot said:

"Great Chief of the Railway, I salute you, O Chief, O Great. I am pleased with railway key, opening road free to me. Its wonderful power to. open the road shows the greatness of your Chiefness."

Now that the marvelous railroad had been constructed through the dark and forbidding mountains to the Pacific Coast, the Mounties had to maintain order along it. In the United States an epidemic of train robberies was plaguing the rail lines. Express cars were blown open and mail clerks killed. Holdup men like Jesse James could outwit the cleverest sheriff or posse.

American railroad executives foresaw constant robbing of the new Canadian Pacific. Outlaws, they predicted, would have a field day. The route was through hundreds of miles of lonely canyons and uplands, where trains had to travel at slow bell. The situation was made to order for holdup men.

But these predictions overlooked one factor—the Northwest Mounted Police. Bandits did not want on their trail the men in crimson and gold who never gave up.

Only once on the new Canadian Pacific did train robbers risk challenging the Mounties. Three outlaws from south of the boundary held up a passenger limited near Kamloops, in the Coastal Range of British Columbia. They disappeared into the blackness of the wilderness night.

Sergent Wilson of the Mounted and six Constables soon were in pursuit. Within forty-eight hours they came upon three men camped beside a river.

"Who are you?" asked the Sergeant.

"We're gold prospectors," answered William Dunn, who had planned the train robbery.

"You don't look like prospectors to me," said Sergeant Wilson. "You look like three men who probably held up the Canadian Pacific train in Kamloops."

"Look out, boys! It's all up!" Dunn shouted to his companions and reached for his revolver.

Sergeant Wilson got to his pistol first. He purposely winged Dunn only in the leg, so he would live to stand trial for train robbery. Within a few days of the time the train had been held up, the three bandits were locked in jail by the Mounties. The train crew identified them and they went to prison. After this, outlaws left the Canadian Pacific Railroad alone.

But the "Idaho Kid" did not know of the reputation of the scarlet police when he galloped across the border into the railroad town of Weyburn, Saskatchewan.

Pulling out his shooting irons, he sprayed the community with lead. Bulbs popped to pieces in street lamps. Glass vanished in store windows. Holes appeared in hats on citizens' heads. One of these citizens, braver than his fellows, announced he would wire for the Mounted Police

Constable in the nearby town of Halbrite, off to the southeast.

"I'll bet twenty-five dollars no tin soldier's going to lock me up," boasted the gunman from Idaho. "I'm boss of this here town. I've got half the sheriffs in Idaho and Montana afraid of me."

Halbrite was on the route of the Canadian Pacific, too, and soon Constable Lett of the Mounted Police clambered down from a caboose in the Weyburn freight yards.

"Where is he?" the Mountie inquired of the first person he met.

The citizen evidently knew exactly whom the Mountie meant. He gestured toward Weyburn's leading hotel, where the "Idaho Kid" had taken over the fanciest suite.

Constable Lett went up the steps two at a time. He tested the lock on the door of the room occupied by the "Idaho Kid." It was fastened. The Mountie took a run at the door and broke it down with his shoulder. As he catapulted into the room, a shot rang out. Apparently it missed, for a terrible commotion could be heard by people in the hotel lobby. Furniture banged on the floor and against the walls in the room of the "Idaho Kid." Once a shriek of pain penetrated to the floors below. Plaster was jarred from the ceilings.

Then two men staggered out across the splintered threshold of the hotel's main suite. Both were spattered with blood. Their faces were red and gory. One of the men was the "Idaho Kid." He wore handcuffs. The other man was Constable Lett of the Mounted Police. He had already arrested the "Idaho Kid" in the name of the Crown for disturbing the peace.

That night a citizen of Weyburn made the "Idaho Kid" very unhappy. The citizen visited the jail and asked the desperado to pay the twenty-five dollars he owed him for betting that a "tin soldier" would never lock up the "Idaho Kid."

And so law and order came to the Canadian Pacific, the

wonderful railway which was to unite Canada as one nation, from the Atlantic's shores to the tossing surf of the Pacific.

Today, when I ride on the Dominion Limited through the passes that split the high mountains, I think of the Mounties who helped push the tracks past the final frontier.

The deep bray of the whistle of the great Diesel-electric locomotive echoes back from the crags. I look out the window and see the lights of the train reflected in a polka-dot pattern on nearby cliffs. We span a gorge with a rumble. Water roars far below. I flip off the lamps in my bedroom and I can make out jagged summits of snow and ice, towering like sentinels above the railroad.

The red and green twinkle of signal lanterns suddenly appears outside my window in the train. We are coming to a town. A roundhouse for engines is off at the side of the main line. Our wheels click merrily over switches. I see a station surrounded by flowerbeds of geraniums and peonies. This is Revelstoke, division point in the Selkirk region.

Beside the station stands a square-jawed Mountie with broad shoulders and erect posture. He wears a tunic of chocolate-brown, now the standard uniform of the force for every day except holidays and dress occasions. A swagger stick is under his arm. On his head a tall Stetson hat comes to a sharp peak, like a cowboy's sombrero.

But the badges and buttons of this Mountie are the

same, I know, as those worn by the Mounties of old. Each of them proclaims, in French, the traditional motto: "Uphold the Right."

In my mind's eye I glimpse a shadowy company in the mountain twilight behind this young Constable of the modern force. They all are there in the dusk. Sergeant Fury guards the log bridge, while behind him, Superintendent Steele comes staggering from his sick bed. Sergeant Colebrook is falling dead at the feet of Almighty Voice. Assistant Commissioner Macleod is once more making peace with the fierce Blackfeet. Inspector Allen defies Sitting Bull in his own camp. Constable Lett is single-handedly braving the six-shooters of the "Idaho Kid," and off in the distance is the thin red line of Mounties who charged the *Metis* guns at Duck Lake and Cut Knife Hill.

If it had not been for such pioneers in scarlet and gold, no railroad would thread through the majestic ranges which loom above Revelstoke. I still am thinking of these pioneer Mounties, who cleared the way for the Canadian Pacific, as our train gathers speed and heads toward Craigellachie, where the last iron spike was pounded long ago.

6

The Wilderness Police and the Gold Rush

THE KLONDIKE GOLD RUSH IN THE YEAR 1897 WAS A SU-preme test for the Northwest Mounted Police.

A white man named Carmack, married to a Siwash squaw, struck the vein of gold which was to become known as Bonanza Creek. It was one of the greatest mother lodes of all time. Greed gripped men and women everywhere in the world when the steamer *Portland* reached Seattle with $700,000 worth of Klondike nuggets in the ship's safe.

These people abandoned families and jobs. Into the Yukon they rushed, eager to get rich in a hurry. *Chee-chakos*, the Indians called the newcomers. This meant "tenderfeet." And tenderfeet they truly were, completely lacking in knowledge of the fierce sub-Arctic realm they were entering.

They sloshed ashore from ships in thin sweaters and cotton trousers. On the terrible icy staircase of Chilkoot Pass they froze and starved. Some stumbled into the depths below. A man with food in his duffel bag might be murdered on the Alaskan side of the line for a slab of bacon. Beans sold at Dawson City for $1.50 a pound. Eggs often brought five dollars a dozen. A seller could name his own price for beefsteak.

Soon the lonely Yukon teemed with 40,000 brawling, quarreling souls. "You just can't tell lies about the Klondike!" a returning prospector exclaimed to an editor at *The New York Times.* "It's all true!" And the frantic race for riches started again when a clerk in the gold fields was said to have panned $61,000 during a single day.

In the midst of this frenzy were 254 Mounties. Their task seemed impossible. They had no records, no regular courts, no jails. People were nameless. Few had any next of kin closer than a thousand miles away. If somebody disappeared, who knew it?

A police detachment was anchored to the wind-swept crest of the Chilkoot. This was the border between Alaska and the Yukon Territory of Canada. Constables staggered from tent to tent, guided by ropes. Otherwise they might be blown away in the howling blizzards. In one day six feet of snow fell to earth. At some places the drifts were seventy feet deep!

When I was in the North with the American Army, I struggled up Chilkoot Pass in the company of an adventurous Catholic priest, Father Edgar Gallant. From half a century before, splintered lumber and smashed dishes still littered the rocks. Even on a clear and balmy day, the ascent was hard. It seemed unbelievable that men could have climbed those steep slopes in the heavy snows, carrying on their backs the supplies and equipment necessary to erect a police post at the summit. Yet that is what the

Mounties did in the winter of 1898, under Inspector Bobby Belcher.

"Hats off to the valiant red coats!" said Father Gallant, as we looked at the bleak ridge where the police post had been.

"Amen," I replied with feeling.

When the people in the gold rush came to the top of the Chilkoot, the Mounties turned them back if they did not have enough grub. It seemed cruel and heartless, but it was better for the *cheechakos* never to get a nugget than to perish of hunger on the way to the creeks. Furthermore, a starving man might be tempted to kill a person with a knapsack full of food.

On the Canadian side of Chilkoot Pass, the gold-seekers built wooden boats for the long voyage down the Yukon River to the Klondike. This was a place where the Mounties might have some control over the stampeding thousands headed for the diggings. An order went out from police headquarters:

"All barges, rowboats and canoes will be numbered and registered in a book."

The Mounties set up a barricade at the roaring Whitehorse Rapids. Boats full of hurrying but inexperienced tenderfeet would enter this foaming stretch of the Yukon. There would be a sudden drop into a thundering chute. The boat would be hurled broadside to the current and then overturned. The people would be swept into a whirlpool, never to be seen alive again.

Only authorized river pilots now would be allowed to take boats through the rapids, said the Mounties. One of these pilots had been a curly-haired young man from San Francisco named Jack London, who would write many famous books about the gold rush.

Women and children could not ride the dangerous rapids at all. They had to walk the five miles around the white-capped waters under police protection. When a pretty blonde bride fell into the river from the trail, she arrived in the village of Whitehorse wearing the red jacket and gold-striped breeches of a Mountie! The only clothes she owned had been drenched in the Yukon.

Dawson was the center of the stampede for gold. Until the Mounties came, it was the wildest and wickedest place in North America. Gamblers and pickpockets and evil women preyed on the miners who had chamois-skin pouches full of gold dust.

After the arrival of the Mounties, things were different. When a drunken *cheechako* struck his wife, a Corporal of police set him to work on the woodpile, sawing and splitting timber in sub-zero weather. A Constable grabbed by the scruff of the neck a nimble little man he glimpsed putting his hand in another man's pocket. The woodpile for him! Prisoners toiled until their arms ached and their backs were sore. They split 1,000 cords of wood in one winter.

"It is a bitter medicine, but it will discourage violence and thievery," said Superintendent Steele, the same

Mountie who had stopped the riot on the Canadian Pacific line in the Selkirk Mountains.

The work of the Mounted Police in the Klondike was made especially hard by the fact that there was no check on evildoers across the boundary in Alaska. In fact, Alaska had not even been organized as a territory, and criminals ranged in search of the products of other men's toil.

It was the year 1898, and as Inspector Zac Wood of the Northwest Mounted Police slogged on snowshoes through a lane of evergreen trees, he wondered if he would run into any of these birds of prey. A robust man, he was wearing a hairy coat of buffalo hide, fastened with leather straps and metal buttons. Over his shoulders were two large kitbags. These must have been heavy, for Zac Wood bent beneath the burden.

Snow coated the boughs of spruce and pine. The Inspector's webbed footgear made a hissing noise as he slid along, gently swinging his arms for balance.

Now he studied the steep slopes above the trail. "Avalanche weather," he called over his shoulder to the two Constables who followed him.

The warm Chinook winds from the nearby sea made the Inspector unloosen his greatcoat. He knew that the ice and shale on the rugged sides of Chilkoot Pass might soon be melted from their frozen perch. Already the Mounties had dug out the bodies of seventy-one seekers for gold. They had been crushed in a landslide which had swept through the narrow slot of the pass.

But Inspector Wood had more to worry about than avalanches. In kitbags and dunnage sacks he and his Constables carried $150,000 in gold ingots. The police in the Klondike had collected these funds as customs duties. Now they had to get the money to government vaults in Victoria, 1,200 miles off to the south.

In Skagway, the Alaskan port which was the entrance to the Klondike, waited a man named Jefferson Smith. He was commonly called "Soapy," but this harmless nickname cloaked the fact that he was Alaska's most feared bandit. And Alaska had no police force, no sheriffs, no organized law-enforcement at all. With slight risk to himself, "Soapy" robbed scores of people on their way to and from the gold diggings.

But would "Soapy" and his gang dare tangle with the Northwest Mounted Police? The question was about to be answered. What prize could be more tempting to an outlaw than $150,000? It was reported that "Soapy" had learned what Inspector Wood carried in his kitbags.

Many generations had gone into the erect bearing and fine features of Inspector Zac Wood. He was a nephew of Jefferson Davis, who had led the Confederate States in the American Civil War. The Inspector also was a grandson of General Zachary Taylor, known to his troops as "Old Rough and Ready," who in 1848 had been elected President of the United States.

Yet a direct descendant of a President was in keeping with the best traditions of the Northwest Mounted. Had

In kitbags and dunnage sacks they carried $150,000 in gold.

not Francis J. Dickens, a son of the famous author Charles Dickens, risen to be an Inspector in the scarlet-coated force during the bloody fighting of the Riel Rebellion?

As quiet Inspector Zac Wood, grandson of the twelfth American President, neared the beach at Dyea, he gave a final heft to the precious kitbags over his stout shoulders. He was determined that the funds should reach the strong-box of the steamer *Tartar* which, even then, waited at the wharf in Skagway.

The Mounties had no power on Alaskan soil. But to have entrusted the fortune in gold to anyone except the wilderness police would have merely resulted in handing it over to "Soapy" Smith and his gang.

At the foot of Chilkoot Pass, the police put across the bay in a rowboat. They pulled hard on the oars. An icy wind stung their hands and faces. Suddenly they saw a larger boat headed for them. It was full of men with grim expressions. It seemed about to ram their smaller craft.

Zac Wood unlimbered his carbine. He aimed it at the other boat. "Lay to or I shoot!" he called.

The boat continued on its course. The Inspector sighted down the barrel of the gun. At the final instant before a collision, the second boat veered off in a surge of spray. The Mounties sighed with relief. They had no desire to leave their bones at the bottom of that cold bay.

And now Inspector Wood and his men were carrying the gold onto the Skagway docks. "Soapy" Smith himself leaned against a timbered piling. Members of his gang eyed the Mounties menacingly. It was a tense moment. The outlaw and the Inspector of police looked each other straight in the face. Armed sailors from the crew of the *Tartar* stood on deck, ready to help defend the gold.

"Soapy" Smith knew the Mounties would die there on the wharf before they surrendered the money belonging to the Canadian government. Some of those who tried to take the money would die with them. This prospect was not pleasing to "Soapy."

And so it was the outlaw whose nerve broke first. He grinned at Zac Wood. "Ah, Inspector," he smiled, "we would be honored if you visited us in Skagway for a few days. It is a most delightful place."

Zac Wood looked at Skagway's bleak shacks and frowzy saloons. He grinned back. "Your kind invitation is appreciated," he replied with mock courtesy. "But we have urgent business elsewhere."

The Mounties trudged up the *Tartar's* gangplank. The whistle of the steamer bounced off the cliffs above the docks. The *Tartar* backed out into the channel, and the gold was on the way to safety. A little band of Mounties had whisked this glittering prize under the noses of the most desperate cutthroats in Alaska.

The Indians, too, presented the Mounties with problems. Into the police post at Pleasant Camp on the border rushed a breathless American missionary, the Reverend Sellon. He announced that Chilkat Indians in the tribal village of Klukwan were torturing to death a ten-year-old boy named Kodik.

"Only you men of the Northwest Mounted can save him," gasped the preacher. "Oh, please come, please come!"

Constable Leeson faced a stern choice. The Northwest Mounted had no legal right to stop a crime from being committed on Alaskan soil. Yet there were things more important than legal rights! Could he allow a boy to be killed by torture?

The Mountie began ripping off his scarlet tunic. He called to Constables Brown and Simpson to do likewise.

"We'll go in our old trail clothes, without uniforms," said Leeson. "That will make it a little less official. But we're going to go!"

The Mounties slipped revolvers and extra ammunition into their mackinaw pockets. They hurried along the fir-bordered path behind the missionary.

At Klukwan they found the Indian village silent. By the silvery light of the moon, the preacher pointed to a tumbledown house where poor Kodik had been tortured.

The Mounties entered and heard groans of pain from beneath the floor. They ripped up the boards and found little Kodik. He had been scalded with steam from a boiling kettle. Sharp sticks had made gaping wounds in his chest. Cords had cut his wrists. And now the Chilkats had gone away to let him die of cold and hunger, in a dark hole under the floor.

"Why have the Indians done this?" asked Leeson.

"They suspect Kodik of witchcraft," explained the Reverend Sellon. "One of their chiefs is sick. An ignorant witch-doctor claims that Kodik has put a curse on the chief. It is the way the witch-doctor accounts for his own failure to cure the chief's illness."

Angry murmurs were now heard in Klukwan. Some of the Chilkats were returning to look at their victim. Fury rippled among the Indians when they discovered that Kodik had been rescued. They would kill Kodik and his rescuers, too!

But never did Indians shiver as the cowardly Chilkats shivered when they learned who the tall man was who stood at the side of the missionary! The dreaded scarlet police had come from across the border. What medicine-man could match magic such as this?

"Perhaps," whined Yiltcock, another chief, "we of the Chilkat Tribe have been sorely mistaken. It may be that the boy Kodik is not guilty of witchcraft, after all."

While the Indians stood aside meekly, Constable Leeson carried the sobbing, tortured Kodik up the trail to the police post at Pleasant Camp. There he was bandaged and fed wholesome food. The little boy got well and eventually was sent to a school for native children in Sitka.

The reputation of the Mounties for upholding the right was spreading throughout the world. Returning *cheechakos* said that only the troopers in red coats had kept the Klondike from flaming with violence every day and night.

Edward VII, King of England, decided that so great a police organization should be honored by the throne. The Crown would be pleased to recognize the Mounties as of "Royal" quality. And so in the year 1904 the name of the force became the Royal Northwest Mounted Police, by order of the monarch of the British Empire!

Typical of the deeds which earned this honor was the solving of the most fiendish killings ever to take place in the Yukon.

Along a backwater of the river near Bonanza Creek, Corporal Storm Piper discovered the body of a man who had been shot through the head. A tag on a metal key ring showed that the dead man was a French-Canadian from distant Quebec.

Constable Jack Burns of the Mounted could talk French fluently. In plain clothes, he roamed among the French-speaking people in the gold fields. The murdered man turned out to be Leon Bouthillette, a carpenter who had taken his life's savings and gone to the Yukon to strike it rich.

Over the backwoods telegraph line which had just been erected, the Mounties got off a wire to Bouthillette's home in Quebec. People there had heard from him in Vancouver, where he had fallen in with two old friends, Alphonse Constantin and Guy Beaudoin. All were off for the Yukon together.

And now the numbering of the boats proved its value. Bouthillette and his pals had voyaged down the Yukon

River from the lakes near Chilkoot Pass in boat Number 3744. But two other men had been in the boat, making a total of five passengers. Still more important, boat Number 3744 had never reached Dawson.

And then Beaudoin's body was found in the river, likewise shattered by a blast from a shotgun.

This was a case the Mounties had to break. The Yukon buzzed with terror. Men were walking around with fortunes in gold dust in their pockets. But if the slayers of

Bouthillette and Beaudoin were at large, would anyone be safe?

The Mounties ran the Yukon mail by dog sled. At every cabin and camp, they asked about boat 3744 and who had been in it. Finally the boat was discovered, tied to a poplar tree beside the river. Mounties talked to carpenters and at last found two men in Whitehorse who had built boat 3744. They told the police of a pair of young French-Canadians, who were with Bouthillette and his friends when the boat was bought.

The descriptions perfectly matched those of two noisy travelers who had been in Dawson. Their names were Fournier and LaBelle. Constable Burns, gossiping with many French-Canadians, decided that these men had been in boat 3744 with the Bouthillette party.

A dance-hall hostess helped lead the Mountie to Fournier, whom he arrested on suspicion of murder.

But LaBelle was needed to seal the case, and LaBelle had fled the Yukon. Where was he? He might be anywhere in the world.

Without LaBelle, the case against Fournier fell flat. All evidence pointed to two men as having done away with Leon Bouthillette and his unfortunate comrades.

W. H. Welsh, a plain-clothes detective in the Mounted Police, had an idea. LaBelle had worked in construction camps. These could be a clever place to hide. The Mountie would visit all sorts of construction projects in the Northwest, searching for LaBelle.

But first he had to know just what LaBelle looked like. From the Klondike, Inspector Zac Wood sent one of the boat-builders, a carpenter named Rooke. He could recognize LaBelle on sight.

Welsh and Rooke wandered through the American West. The Mountie detective had papers in his pocket allowing him to arrest LaBelle on United States soil, if he ever found him. Montana, California, Oregon, Utah— these were the states the Mountie scoured, but no La-Belle.

A railroad was being thrust across the Nevada desert. Welsh would make still another try. His orders were not to give up until he returned with LaBelle.

Posing as a timekeeper, Rooke went from tent to tent. In the last tent on the project he saw the man he knew to be LaBelle. And LaBelle felt the cold bracelets of doom when Welsh, the Mountie detective, fastened handcuffs on his wrists.

On the long voyage back to the Klondike, LaBelle broke down and confessed that he and Fournier had killed a total of four prospectors, including Bouthillette and his friends. All the murders were to get the money carried by the dead men, whose bodies were pitched into the Yukon.

"How'd you ever know we were the ones who did it?" LaBelle asked the Mountie.

"A tab on a key ring and a boat number told us," the detective answered.

LaBelle may still have been thinking about this reply as

he and Fournier stood on the hangman's gallows in the barracks square at Dawson, on a grim January morning in the year 1903 when the temperature registered 53 degrees below zero.

It was a case which aroused great respect for the Mounties. Through the North rustled the whisper that the wilderness police never gave up. The pursuit might take them to foreign lands, but it was followed to the end.

7

The Patrol That Never Came Back

THE MOUNTIE PATROL WAS LOST.

Every ravine and gully looked the same. No landmark guided them. Were they still in the valley of the Peel River? Had they reached the Little Wind River or the Hart River? Could they have stumbled so far off their course that they were in the wild watershed of the Bonnet Plume?

And it was cold—a piercing, clawing cold which tore through fur clothing and raked a man's vital organs. One of the Constables stumbled in the snow. He rose to his feet slowly and painfully. It was getting harder to lift one webbed snowshoe past the other.

When a man didn't have enough to eat, the cold did something to him. It stole his strength and robbed him of the will to endure and go on.

Indeed, on this dim, glassy morning as the Inspector peered at his thermometer, he noted that the mercury recorded 56 degrees below frost. This was nearly 90 degrees of frost, for the freezing point lay at 32 degrees above the zero mark.

No wonder that the poor sled dogs bled at the mouth as they strained to pull in the creaking leather harness!

No wonder that a man's fingers trembled and then stiffened if he took off his mittens just to brush a speck from his eye. No wonder that faces began to hurt and ache the instant that masklike scarfs were rolled down.

It was cold, cold, cold. Sometimes they felt willing to offer a year's pay for one warm and balmy hour.

But they were in a white wilderness, and in that wilderness there was no warmth. Rivers were sheets of ice as rigid as granite. Not a line showed where shore and water met. The creeks were frozen, too. Yet in the creeks lurked hidden springs which never hardened. When a man broke through into one of these wet pockets, the party had to stop and build a fire to thaw him out.

This cost them precious time. It also weakened the vigor of the man who had been soaked. He moved along on snowshoes more slowly. Often he was unsteady. This was when the Constable fell in the trail.

But was it the trail?

Behind them they could see the paw marks of the dogs and the woven pattern of their own snowshoes. In front of them stretched an unbroken mantle of white. They might have been on the trail to Dawson, and yet they could be staggering up another creek which led into the blind alley of a box canyon.

Francis J. Fitzgerald, Inspector in His Majesty's Royal Northwest Mounted Police, was learning what Rudyard Kipling had meant when the famous poet wrote of Canada, as "Our Lady of the Snows."

Snow! Snow! Snow!

Everywhere there was snow, but no landmark to guide them. Fitzgerald had made the patrol once before. He had made it from Dawson to Fort McPherson. And now he was headed in the opposite direction, with Dawson as the goal. Strangely enough, all the features of the landscape seemed different. And who had bargained for the worst winter since white men mapped the North Country?

The maps were sketchy, too. In fact, the Mounties had decided to reach Dawson by the Blackstone River Divide, and of this route they had no map at all. Not even the compass served them in that twisting maze of hills and ridges and snowy peaks.

It was one of the duties of the Mounted Police to establish a line of travel and communication in the Arctic. This called for a journey by dog sled across the bleak height of land separating the two great rivers of the North, the Yukon and the Mackenzie.

The patrol threaded through the desolate region between Dawson in the Klondike and Fort McPherson above the Arctic Circle. It covered 510 lonely miles. Ordinarily the journey took a month of stubborn mushing by dog sled. Once, however, Constable Forrest had dashed from Dawson to McPherson in three weeks. This was still the record.

The patrol carried mail. It also brought the dispatches and reports for the Commissioner of the force. And it maintained contact between the main northern districts of the Mounted Police.

Fitzgerald, a dashing Irishman, commanded the Mackenzie River sub-district at Fort McPherson. He had an ambition. It was to beat Forrest's time on the annual patrol.

More than once Fitzgerald said to companions, "There's a way to make it faster than Forrest did—travel light!"

Grizzled northerners frequently shook their heads at this, but Fitzgerald insisted, "It's a patrol, not a freight line. They pack too much cargo."

And now Fitzgerald was traveling light. He had pared down the quantities of flour, bacon, beans, and tinned beef usually taken by the patrol. Three subordinates were along with him. Constables George Kinney and Richard Taylor were young members of the force, able to break trail tirelessly. The guide was Special Constable Sam Carter. He once had made the trip with Forrest, the Mountie who held the record.

This had disturbed the Reverend Whittaker, who was the minister of the little log Anglican Church at the fort. "Take an Indian as your guide, Inspector," he had urged. "Remember—white men have been in this rough and rugged country only a comparatively short time."

"Indians don't make enough speed on the trail, Reverend," said the Mountie commandant.

But the pastor's plea had made some impression. Fitzgerald agreed to depend upon Indian Esau as far as

Mountain Creek. After that, the patrol would be on its own.

They started in the gray gloom of a dawn that was like most December mornings north of the Circle. Their caravan consisted of three dog sleds, with five yelping Huskies to each sled. The men at the post wished there had been a few more dogs. One trooper was worried because the Inspector had recently used the same animals on a mission across the ice of the Arctic Ocean from Herschel Island.

"Those dogs aren't rested—they ought to be a lot

fresher and livelier," said Corporal Somers. "They haven't any pep. Their tails seem to be dragging already."

But on New Year's Day, 1911, the patrol was at Mountain Creek. They had made fair time. It still was possible to match Forrest's record, although they had been forced to go out of their way around pools of open water on the frozen rivers.

Fitzgerald explained to Esau that the white men could proceed without further help. Their sleds carried barely enough food for four weeks. The Indian grunted and made ready to leave them.

As he packed his bedding and duffel, Esau asked Carter: "Does Special Constable know right trail?"

"Sure thing," replied Carter. "All the way into Dawson."

But Carter was wrong.

The men, instead of speeding ahead, were harried by constant delay—delay while they searched for the route. From Little Wind River, Carter could not find the canyons which led to the Blackstone watershed. Once over the Blackstone Divide, the going would be easy to the Mounted Police detachment at Forty-Mile and then on to Dawson.

But where was the Blackstone?

They crossed windswept plateaus without trees, and it was getting colder. For the first time Fitzgerald noticed that the grub was low. Had it been a grim mistake to travel light?

On January 11, the day on which they should have been in Dawson if they were to equal Constable Forrest's record, they were still locked in a white and trackless wilderness.

In the Inspector's mind a desperate decision was taking form. He had with him the only law-enforcement officers in the vast area. These men had to survive to "uphold the right." It was important to complete the patrol. But it was more important that the Mounties of the Fort Mc-Pherson detachment not be wiped out.

On January 17 Fitzgerald had made up his mind. "Boys," he said, "we're going back to McPherson."

Tears came to Carter's eyes. He had failed the Inspector and he had failed the force. He had lost the way to Dawson. Now, could he get them home to McPherson?

That night the Inspector wrote carefully in his police diary, which all Mountie officers carried in their kitbags:

"Carter is now completely lost and does not know one river from another. We have only 10 pounds of flour and eight pounds of bacon and some dried fish. I should not have taken Carter's word that he knew the way from Little Wind River."

As Fitzgerald closed the book, he heard the wind sighing mournfully in the trees. The diary was vital, for the 295 miles to McPherson might be impossible for men without food. If they did not return, the Northwest Mounted would find them—dead or alive. Either way, the diary would be with them to tell the force what had happened.

The next day the Inspector pulled out his service revolver and killed one of the dogs. It was his scheme that the men should eat the dried fish. Perhaps the dogs would live on one another. But the dogs refused to eat the dead Husky. Instead, the men had to chew the stringy dog meat, while nausea gripped their stomachs.

Then their troubles seemed to mount more rapidly than before. The weather dropped to 53 degrees below zero. Constable Taylor broke through a hidden spring into icy water to his waist. Three precious hours were lost thawing him out. The Inspector had to kill another dog. He scrawled in his diary:

"Our food is now dog meat and tea. . . . All hands feeling sick, supposed to be from eating dogs' liver."

Fate seemed to be mocking them. It was a winter of no game. If only a woodland caribou would prance within their rifle sights! The thought of the briskets and ribs and steaks of juicy caribou meat nearly drove them wild with hunger.

But that night they ate dog as usual. Now they began to abandon sleds, for the harness was empty. They boiled the greasy harness leather and drank the smelly broth which it made.

In the diary Fitzgerald wrote:

"January 31——62 degrees below. Skin peeling off our faces and parts of the body. Lips all swollen and split."

Yet he still retained a faint glimmer of hope:

"February 3——26 degrees below. Men and dogs very

103

thin and weak. We have traveled about 200 miles on dog meat, and have about 100 miles to go, but I think we will make it all right."

They had started from McPherson with fifteen dogs. Five were left. These thin animals could hardly drag the one remaining sled. Constable Dick Taylor tottered and fell in the trail. He had to crawl half a hundred paces on his knees before he could get to his feet. The Inspector watched him with tears in his eyes.

On February 5 Fitzgerald wrote in the diary for the last time:

"About 48 degrees below. Just after noon I broke through the ice. Found one foot slightly frozen. Killed another dog tonight. . . . Can go only a few miles a day. Everybody breaking out on the body and skin peeling off."

In the Inspector's foot there was no feeling. The flesh was starting to turn black. Without proper nourishment, his body could not combat gangrene and infection. Even if they got back, would amputation confront him? Might he be crippled for life?

But would they get back?

Every inch was a horror now for the Mountie officer. In the slippery snow, his one good foot had to do the work of two. Frequently his snowshoes became entangled and he fell painfully. The others could not help him up, for they could hardly stand on their own feet.

Yet they had not far to go. Carter recognized the Peel

Constable Dick Taylor tottered and fell in the trail.

River once more. Only fifty-five miles to McPherson! They were boiling what was left of the moosehide harness. There might be some slight food value in the dark brown "soup" that remained in the bottom of the kettle.

But Kinney and Taylor could travel no farther. They lay in their sleeping bags, unable to move.

A little dog meat and a powdering of flour remained on the sled. Fitzgerald left it all with the two Constables, who finally had given out.

"We'll send the police from McPherson, boys," he said. "It won't be long until you see them coming around the bend in the river," he said. And he managed a smile.

Kinney smiled back wanly. The two men, once stalwart Constables of the Mounted, were mere skeletons. Their faces looked like skulls. Kinney's feet had frozen and were twice their normal size. Even if Fitzgerald got to McPherson by a miracle and help arrived, George Kinney would never walk again. As he lay there in his bedding, Kinney was only twenty-seven years old, but he had the gaunt appearance of a man of eighty-seven.

And now Fitzgerald and Carter struggled on. At least they did not have to search hard for their back trail. The way was evident. Several times they tottered past deserted shacks used by trappers. The empty windows stared at them coldly. They looked within for grub, but the wolverines had been there first.

Forty miles from McPherson!

Much of the time they were on their hands and knees,

like beasts of the forest. If only Corporal Somers from the post were on patrol! He would save them. But Somers did not come.

Thirty miles from McPherson!

Without enough food, in the cruelest weather white men ever had experienced in the North, they had crawled and staggered nearly 270 miles. Were they to perish almost within sight of the friendly column of smoke from the barracks at McPherson?

Twenty-five miles from McPherson, the two men had used almost the final ounce of their ebbing strength. Carter died, but first he babbled to the Inspector his sorrow over having lost the trail. Fitzgerald covered his friend's face with a faded blue handkerchief and he crossed his shriveled arms on his chest.

The Inspector of police lay helplessly on his back. He remembered the proud day he had enlisted in the Mounted at Regina. He had told his mother that some day he would be an officer in the famous force and wear brass insignia on his shoulders. Well, he had become an officer and his mother was proud of him.

His mother! He had forgotten his mother. Beside him was a charred stick from the fire. He could not find his pencils in the kitbag. The effort of looking was too much for him. On a sheet of paper torn from the diary, he smudged with the black stick:

"All money in dispatch bag and bank, clothes, I leave

to my dearly beloved mother, Mrs. Mary Fitzgerald, Halifax. God bless all. F. J. Fitzgerald, R. N. W. M. P."

He lay back on the unyielding snow, gasping for breath. Presently he was more quiet and his breathing less labored. And then death closed the fading and weary eyes of Francis J. Fitzgerald, Inspector in His Majesty's Royal Northwest Mounted Police.

The snows fell. The wind swayed the spruce boughs. The ice floes heaved and buckled in the Peel River. A grouse fluttered near the edge of the clearing. An antlered caribou stalked over a white hummock.

And after many days, the relief column came from Forty-Mile, as the Inspector had known it would. Indian Charlie Stewart was breaking trail. Corporal Dempster, a veteran of the Arctic, was in command. He had orders from Superintendent Snyder at Dawson to find Fitzgerald at all costs. And he had found him. Previously he had also stumbled on the bodies of Kinney and Taylor.

Dempster took off his muskrat hat in tribute. Back across that terrible wilderness Fitzgerald had struggled for 270 miles, only to die twenty-five miles from McPherson and safety!

But the thing which Dempster noticed above all else was that the Inspector had written with his last failing strength the initials of the force he had served until the tragic and lonely end of his life.

8

Tracking Down an Arctic Mystery

THREE YEARS AMONG THE ESKIMO TRIBES ON THE SHORES
of the Arctic Ocean had taught George Le Roux and
Pierre Rouvier, frontier priests of the Catholic Church,
that a native with Sinnisiak's shifty eyes and sagging jaw
was not to be trusted. Uluksak, the other guide, although
cheerful and willing, seemed a slave of Sinnisiak. He
obeyed his orders without question.

Yet thus far on the journey southward in this year of
1913 there had been no trouble. The four men slogged
along the banks of the Coppermine River, each intent on
keeping his feet in the icy caribou trail. Father Rouvier,
leader of the party, could not see Sinnisiak greedily looking over the piles of goods on the two sleds.

The piles contained guns, ammunition, brightly-colored
blankets, church ornaments, sacred robes, axes and much
grub. This was enough to make an Eskimo rich for life,
the envy of all tribesmen on Coronation Gulf.

Yet for guiding the two missionaries to the-land-where-
little-trees-grow, Sinnisiak and Uluksak were to receive
only a few traps. Why not possess all the great wealth
heaped on the sleds? No eyes were watching—now!

Father Rouvier died on the trail as Sinnisiak's knife

Sinnisiak's knife plunged into his back.

plunged into his back. Father Le Roux, hearing his companion's last startled gasp, rushed for the Winchester .44 rifle which was slipped under the lashings of the larger sled. For an instant there rushed through the priest's mind the warnings they had heard at Fort Norman about the primitive Kogloktogmiuts, a wandering band of Eskimos along the bleak Coppermine River.

"The gun!" Father Le Roux shouted in panic, as he leaped for the duffel on the sleigh.

To him, possession of the rifle suddenly meant life itself. He knew it was loaded and ready to fire.

But Sinnisiak stood nearer, as he had craftily planned. The Eskimo was the first to grab the slender thunderstick. Two bullets ripped through the brave priest's parka of sealskin and into his lungs. Father Le Roux lay choking in the snow. His blood reddened the cold white drifts.

At the command of Sinnisiak, the obedient Uluksak ended the groans of the dying man with an ax. Then Sinnisiak kicked the body to one side of the river trail.

"Come!" snapped Sinnisiak to the other Eskimo.

While Uluksak whimpered in fright, Sinnisiak turned around the heavily-laden sleds. The two natives disappeared in the gloom of the short Arctic daylight, driving the dogs in the direction of the roaming Eskimo tribe camped at the frozen mouth of the Coppermine.

Sinnisiak's barrel-like chest was bursting with pride. His slanting eyes gleamed in satisfaction. He was rich beyond his most fanciful dreams. The treasures on the white men's sleds were his. And who would know of the grim deed that had been done by the river bank?

The hungry wolf packs would come and the Arctic snows would fall—snows which would pelt down for months without stopping. In the spring not a trace of the crime would remain. He and Uluksak were safe. No one ever would find out what had happened to the smiling whites with the long black skirts.

No one?

Once, just once, Sinnisiak looked back furtively over his shoulder, into the darkened south. Had he forgotten something? In his cunning mind he struggled to remember the whisperings he had heard at the council fire about the *Palugtok-angut*, the men in red coats with the head of the buffalo on their gleaming buttons. These men were said to journey by night as well as by day. They also were said to be terrible enemies of evildoers.

And so, for a single fleeting moment, fear traveled with Sinnisiak as he and his partner in murder, Uluksak, pushed into the Arctic twilight. . . .

When people are two years overdue, it is natural to be alarmed. What had happened to Pierre Rouvier and George Le Roux? Father Frapance, of the Oblate Order of priests, penned a letter to the one agency which might be able to locate these long-absent servants of his church.

The letter was read carefully by a tall man with a booming voice and merry blue eyes. On his shoulders glistened bright bits of metal, the insignia of an Inspector in the Mounted Police.

At the age of twenty-six, Charles Deering La Nauze, born in Ireland, was the youngest commissioned officer in "G" Division. The families of the wilderness called him "Denny." He had worked his way up from Constable to Inspector in seven years, starting when he was nineteen. This was unusually fast because promotions in the Mounted Police are hard to earn. Denny always smiled, but behind the smile stood the most fearless manhunter in "G" Division.

"G" Division patrolled the Northwest Territories, a region as large as India. Somewhere in this immense area the mystery of the missing priests was to be unlocked.

"Find out what happened to them, Denny," commanded the Superintendent.

La Nauze was young in years but he knew the North as he knew the fingers of his own hand. He had read countless reports on the Arctic and he had paddled up and down the Three Rivers Country—the Athabaska, the Liard, and the Peace. He referred to Eskimos in the term commonly used by veteran factors of the Hudson's Bay Company. He called them "Huskies."

"I wonder if those 'Huskies' could have done anything to the Fathers," he muttered, as he went over a map of the vast domain where he had to begin his search.

La Nauze rode an old day coach with a pot-bellied stove from Edmonton to Peace River Crossing, the end of the railroad. He shot the foaming rapids of the Peace in a trim Peterborough canoe. When it was too dark to see the swift water, he camped in meadows of fireweed and Indian paintbrush.

By the light of his fire, La Nauze studied notebooks he had filled with words spoken by Indians and Eskimos. He realized that only the native peoples could tell him what had befallen the vanished priests. They alone held the secret. In two years all other evidence must have disappeared.

"I'll probably need an interpreter," La Nauze mused.

When the Inspector reached Fort Smith, the dumpy little sternwheeler *Mackenzie River* had steam up for her once-a-year voyage downstream to the Arctic Ocean.

"Wait!" shouted La Nauze across the water.

He dashed up the gangplank with his knapsack and kitbags, leaving the trusty canoe tied to a wharf.

On the 750-mile voyage the Inspector was nervous and impatient. Each passing day made his task more difficult. What clues were left, even now? He spent hours pacing back and forth in the boat's wheelhouse.

"Can't you go faster?" he asked the skipper.

"Inspector, we're nearly running away from our paddle wheel as it is," the skipper answered.

When the cry of "Wood up!" rang through the boat, the Mountie was the first man on shore to help pass rough slabs of cordwood on deck for the snorting boilers.

Finally the *Mackenzie River* docked at Fort Norman on

the Mackenzie, where men later would drill for oil. On shore stood the trader D'Arcy Arden, last white person to see Fathers Rouvier and Le Roux alive. He introduced the Inspector to Father Frapance from the Norman Mission.

"Inspector La Nauze, we have heard about you," said Father Frapance. "If anyone can find out what has happened to our brothers, we know that you can."

And now to retrace the pilgrimage of the Fathers who had vanished!

The party arranged for a York boat, a flat-bottomed craft built of spruce lumber and manned with long sweeps. This was how men had journeyed in the far reaches of the North almost from the time of Alexander Mackenzie himself, the pioneer head of the Northwest Fur Company.

The route of La Nauze and his companions twisted up the Bear River. The river was so shallow that they had to jump overboard and pull with ropes across their shoulders. Paddles and sweeps could get no leverage; they merely splintered against the rocky bottom.

The water clawed at the ankles of the Inspector and his guides, and it was water fed by melting snow. Legs and feet became numb. The task wore down even Special Constable Ilavernik, a friendly Eskimo who had been on expeditions with the great explorer, Vilhjalmur Stefansson. Ilavernik had been allowed to bring his broad-faced wife when he told La Nauze:

"She sew caribou skins into fine *mukluks*. Put fancy beads on *mukluks*—they keep feet warm when glass stick say sixty below, mebbe colder. They be best *mukluks* in whole Nort' Country."

The tall Mountie grinned at the Eskimo's wife. "All right, all right." He laughed. "Maybe good cook, too—huh?"

Ilavernik would be the interpreter. Few white men spoke the jerky tongue of the Kogloktogmiut Tribe. Fathers Rouvier and Le Roux had mastered the Kogloktogmiut lingo, but where were they?

And the wind sighing in the treetops was the only answer.

One peril was followed by another. With the river surmounted, La Nauze's party was on Great Bear Lake. Gales whipped the huge fresh-water sea into a whirlpool of froth and spume. Great Bear Lake is more than 300 miles across and its waves can be higher than a ship's mainmast.

For eleven days La Nauze waited in the protection of an inlet. Then he could delay no longer. The trail already was only a ragged thread. Did it lead anywhere?

"Let's go," he said. "This is it!"

On Great Bear Lake they rowed for their lives. It was summer but a few ice floes as big as pianos still tossed on the lake near shore. These threatened to crush the wooden boat. The water nipped at the passengers with chilly fangs. The bottom of the craft was always awash. Their food was constantly soaked. The skin on their hands peeled off from the steady wetting.

They were weary and shivering by the time they tottered into D'Arcy Arden's tiny trading post on the northern rim of Great Bear Lake. The calendar in the pocket of La Nauze's mackinaw read only September 20, but the Arctic winter was closing in early. There could be no attempt at the Height of Land which blocked them off from the Coppermine River, until spring came with its releasing Chinook winds.

While the others built a rude cabin of pine logs, the Inspector and Father Frapance snowshoed for nine days to reach Lake Rouvier, where the missing priests had hoped to construct a mission school for native children.

La Nauze found a rustic shelter—deserted. He entered with his flashlight and discovered Bibles, rosaries and other articles a missionary would not have left behind for long. The bindings and papers of the Holy books were mildewed by weather.

"No human being has crossed this threshold for many, many months—that's clear," said the Mountie.

The door of the hut was off its hinges. The empty windows stared vacantly. Wolverines and other beasts had gnawed at the boards. Cans of beans and soup had been bitten by sharp teeth. La Nauze gathered this evidence into his duffel bag.

It was apparent that Fathers Rouvier and Le Roux had never returned after their original departure. Foul play must have occurred. Were they dead? La Nauze suspected the worst.

"I don't like the looks of it, Father Frapance," he said to his companion. "An accident might have happened to one of them, but hardly likely to both. I'm beginning to think they may have been murdered."

Father Frapance crossed himself and murmured a prayer.

The Inspector and his party spent an uncomfortable winter. Whitefish, hooked through the thick ice, were their principal diet. Frequently the temperature stood at 65 degrees below zero. When a man spit, the moisture crackled in mid-air and was practically frozen when it hit the ground. The furry sled dogs whimpered in their holes in the snow and begged for the warmth of the cabin.

On Christmas Day the good-natured wife of Ilavernik gave them all beautiful *mukluks* of caribou hide. These were cozy moccasins with tops like leggings. Beads decorated the moccasins in patterns which resembled bears and seals. La Nauze hung empty tin cups and spoons on a little spruce to make a Christmas tree. The white men sang *Silent Night, Holy Night* while the Eskimo couple swayed their dark heads to the gentle tune.

The Inspector lifted his metal mug in a toast. "To our loved ones, far away," he said.

La Nauze scarcely recognized himself. The 26-year-old Mountie had grown a heavy beard to protect his face from the cruel temperatures. Even with this mat of hair on his chin and cheeks, he could feel the cold biting at him as if it had teeth.

In the spring Father Frapance returned to his mission at Fort Norman, which he could neglect no longer.

And now La Nauze finally was on the trail. Somewhere, across the Arctic Divide, lay the secret of what had happened to the two priests.

With Ilavernik and the Inspector taking turns at breaking trail for the floundering Husky dogs, the party struggled over the jagged ridge separating the watersheds of the Dease and Coppermine Rivers. Snow still blanketed the land, although they knew it was balmy by this time off to the distant south.

La Nauze had been gone from civilization for a year, with no word of his family or friends. Across the sea, the British and the Imperial troops of the German Kaiser were locked in a dreadful war. Who was winning? La Nauze wondered.

It took thirty days of stubborn sledding across the barrens to get to the coast. Not a stick grew in that region; there were not even any stunted trees or any bushes. La Nauze and his companions were in a frozen desert. Unable to build a fire, they gobbled their meat and fish raw. At night they huddled together to keep warm.

The wind cut like a blade through the fur parkas which hooded their heads and reached nearly to their knees. Without the *mukluks* sewed by Ilavernik's willing Eskimo wife, their feet soon would have frozen. Their precious mittens hung on stout cords, so they never would be lost in the snow.

La Nauze's red Mounted Police jacket, with its blue collar and gold braid, lay folded carefully in the pile of baggage on one of the sleds. This frigid prairie was no place for pomp and ceremony! The scarlet tunic always could be put on under his furs when a show of authority was needed.

La Nauze felt his strength slipping away. Yet he had to keep on. He had a duty to perform.

The day came when he drove his dog team straight into a band of threatening Kogloktogmiuts on the Polar shore. He prodded Ilavernik to begin asking questions. Had they seen two white men? Where were they now? Had they been harmed?

The Eskimos grunted angrily but some of them were nervous. Even in that wild and remote place, they had heard of the *Palugtok-angut*, who would pursue evil to the ends of the earth. Obviously, a man who came with such power was one of the *Palugtok-angut*, the crimson police.

Most of that summer of 1916 La Nauze roamed the ragged edge of the Arctic Ocean. He sat at tribal fires and he went on hunts for fierce white bears with dripping red mouths. His mission took genuine patience. He had to know when to grin and laugh with these simple people. He had to know when to grab a stubborn chief by the throat and demand a straight reply.

Once, with Kogloktogmiut knives pointed at his back, La Nauze steadfastly told a medicine-man:

"If aught happens to us, the scarlet police will come.

They will not be few, as we are, but as many as the grains of the sand on the shores of the sea when the snow and ice are gone in the-month-of-much-sunshine."

The Eskimos heard and a murmur rippled around the council. What a quantity of bright buttons with the head of the buffalo would be needed to dress all these *Palugtok-angut*!

Week after week went by. The Inspector feared it might be a hopeless quest. But he could never return to the headquarters of "G" Division without the answer to this

riddle—not if he had to question every tribesman in the Northwest Territories.

In a village near Cape Lambert, far beyond the Arctic Circle, Ilavernik trembled one night with great excitement. "They tell me who killed the priests," he whispered hoarsely. "The priests, they very good to this village. They help cure a terrible sickness that makes bumps on the face. These people much angry with the bad Eskimos who kill the priests."

"Where are the bad men?" asked Ilavernik.

A chieftain with short, scraggly whiskers pointed northward. "Ten sleeps," he said.

By this time La Nauze's little band had been reinforced by the arrival of Corporal Wyndham V. Bruce. He had sledded almost 1,000 bleak miles from the Mounted Police post at Herschel Island, then the farthest north of any garrison in the world.

They lashed the dogs over the frozen ocean and onto Victoria Land. They were in the Polar ice pack, in the latitude of the North Magnetic Pole. The chase had taken them nearly to the very top of the globe.

La Nauze now was being guided by the writings of Sir John Franklin. He was a daring explorer who had disappeared with his crew and sailing ship in this ghostly realm of ice almost a century earlier.

The Mounties were in a place where few white men had ever been before. "Wonder if we'll ever get home," said Bruce.

"Home!" exclaimed La Nauze, echoing the beloved word.

But the pursuit was at its climax.

In a sealskin hut crouched Sinnisiak. A priest's robe covered his moccasins. He reached for a gun, the gun that had shot Father Rouvier several years earlier. The Inspector grabbed him by the shoulder. Sinnisiak dropped the rifle.

Handcuffs clinked suddenly but they would be used only a short time. Sinnisiak would not escape. The bracelets of iron were helpful mainly to show that the white man's law had spanned river and ridge, salt water and fresh.

And the Kogloktogmiut families who howled mournfully outside the hut would never forget the wilderness police who had come from a far region to take away Sinnisiak.

Many times on the patrol, La Nauze had found himself surrounded by Eskimos. A stockade of hostile faces would be all about him. Perhaps a hunting knife or an ugly harpoon would be waved. Then it was important not to flinch or waver. At the first sign of weakness or fear, he might go down beneath a tide of rushing men in furs.

But when one man stood against a hundred and did not show faint heart, even the savage spirit was touched. Ilavernik overheard a chieftain mutter, "Kogloktogmiut, him brave too—like scarlet police."

Uluksak, the other murderer, was hunting on a nearby

island in the ice pack. He ran, but the Inspector ran faster. "Do you know why I have come?" asked La Nauze.

"I know," replied Uluksak. "Are you going to kill me?"

"No," said the Inspector, "I shall not kill you. I have come to take you to the home of the Mounted Police in a distant place. There you will be judged for the terrible thing you have done to two kind and brave men who were friends of the Kogloktogmiut people."

A weary, slow journey separated them from the post of the police detachment on Herschel Island, off the soggy Mackenzie delta. And winter again had laid a frosty grip on the Arctic. The wheezing old *Mackenzie River* had long since headed upstream. La Nauze had to wait through a second *Kice-picim*, the period of the mid-winter moon, when the lynx shook with cold in its lair and the blood of the caribou stag froze in its veins.

It was August of the next year, 1917, when the patrol at last was finished. La Nauze stood once more on the railroad platform at Peace River Crossing, waiting for the train to Edmonton and headquarters. With him were Sinnisiak and Uluksak.

"Fire giant!" they gasped in fright when they saw the snorting locomotive.

The startled telegraph operator in the Northern Alberta Railway station clicked away furiously on his key. The outside world wanted to learn what had happened to Fathers Rouvier and Le Roux. Now the tragic truth was unfolded. The two Eskimos had confessed, and their con-

fessions had been taken down by the interpreter, Ilavernik.

La Nauze had been gone from civilization for two years
and four months. He had not seen his family in all that
time. He had traveled 6,500 miles. More than half of this
distance had been by dog sled in weather as brutal as any
experienced by Admiral Peary on his dash to the North
Pole.

And although the bushy beard long since was gone,
people said to him, "Denny, you've changed!"

The young Inspector thought of the bleak tundra and
the howling tribesmen, and he replied gently, "Yes, I
suppose I have."

But through all the years to come, missionaries and
traders and Arctic whalers would be safe when they entered the domain of the Kogloktogmiuts. What Kogloktogmiut warrior ever would fail to remember the long arm
of the wilderness police? That arm had reached out across
time and space from Peace River Crossing and brought
Sinnisiak and Uluksak before the far-off court of the white
man.

And the lesson had been thoroughly learned, even
though La Nauze himself advised mercy for Uluksak and
Sinnisiak because of their primitive ignorance. "They
should not be hanged," he warned. "Perhaps the Eskimos
will be more law-abiding if they discover that we of the
police can be just and kind as well as persistent and
stern."

Although both Inspector La Nauze and Corporal Bruce were destined to rise to great positions in the force, theirs had been only another deed in the routine of Canada's Mounted Police.

Ilavernik was given a gold watch and chain for faithful service. A letter praised his uncomplaining wife for her *mukluks* and cooking. And the commanding officer of the Royal Mounted, Commissioner Perry, said he could not speak "too highly of Inspector La Nauze and his party."

And up and down the Three Rivers Country, natives murmured that Denny La Nauze was really *se-goose*, the ferret, from whom no secret ever could be kept.

But, for the Mounties, it all had been in the day's work—even though this patrol had taken 850 perilous days to complete. The slayers of the priests had to be captured or else the Northwest Territories would become a nest of knives and spears and stolen rifles. The Mounted Police had no other choice.

Denny La Nauze said later, "I would have had to stay at it in the barren lands, even if I had not come back for 1,850 days."

9

The Mounties Conquer the Northwest Passage

CANADA IS THE ONLY COUNTRY IN THE WORLD WHERE EXploration on a wide scale has been undertaken by the police force.

After all, the Canadian nation was a mere five years old when the Mounties first trekked into the West. The organization of a red-coated troop to enforce the law was one of the first acts of the young government. The Mounties not only grew up with the country, they helped to explore and develop that country.

I realized this when I was in the North with General O'Connor, who directed the building of the Alaska Highway. We studied old records and charts of the frontier where our Engineer regiments were to construct a road to get supply trucks to Fairbanks. And who had made those charts and records? It was the Mounties!

As we watched a lofty suspension bridge being thrust across the Peace River, General O'Connor said, "If it hadn't been for the Mounted Police, we would know a lot less about the best route for the highway. They led the Canadian people into much of this wild area."

I still have the map on which Assistant Commissioner Denny La Nauze, the captor of Sinnisiak and Uluksak, traced for me the route taken by Inspector John Moodie and his scarlet-jacketed Constables from Edmonton to the Klondike.

"Find a back door to the Yukon!"

Those were the orders given to Moodie in 1897, and he carried them out. The patrol lasted fourteen months, and the men froze and went hungry and became as thin as lodgepoles. But they made it. And many years later, bulldozers and steam shovels at Fort St. John were building the first land route in history to Alaska over part of Inspector Moodie's pioneer trail.

When two American explorers named Radford and Street were reported to have been slain by Eskimos, the Mounties went to investigate.

Inspector French and Sergeant-Major Caulkin traveled through Arctic fastnesses where few white men ever had been before. They journeyed 5,200 miles in the snow. They had to eat their dogs to keep from starving. But they were more fortunate than poor Inspector Fitzgerald. They sighted a herd of musk oxen before the dog meat gave out.

Inspector French learned that one of the explorers had beaten the Eskimo guides with a leather whip. This had happened when a native guide refused to abandon his sick wife, who could snowshoe no more across the rough ice. After the whipping, the angry Eskimos killed Radford and Street with harpoons.

Inspector French told police headquarters that he be-

The Mounted Police schooner sailed through Polar ice.

lieved the murders had been the fault of the white men. And he gave it as his opinion that no Eskimo should be arrested for what had happened. "The Eskimos were treated cruelly," said the Inspector.

So word spread among the natives that the *Palugtok-angut*, the police with red coats, were not only swift and terrible in catching wrongdoers, but also merciful and fair in dealing with the innocent.

Such patrols as this did more than win the faith and confidence of the Eskimo people. They also helped to tell the facts about Canada—about its animals and trees and fish and coastline. The Mounties brought down from the vast North Country thick diaries full of important details. This often was the first information describing huge sections of the Yukon and Northwest Territories.

Even today Canada continues to be one of the least known of the world's principal countries. And the Mounties still are exploring the land which they police. Now their domain is all of Canada, not merely the Northwest regions.

In 1920 the name of the organization was changed again—"this time for keeps," in the words of one high-ranking officer. On the shoulder straps of every trooper the metal initials were shortened from R. N. W. M. P. to R. C. M. P.

The force became the Royal Canadian Mounted Police, indicating that its authority covered each of Canada's 3,619,616 square miles.

The most remote part of Canada—indeed, the most remote realm of North America—was explored by the
Mounties only a comparatively few years ago. This task
began in June of 1940 at the busy seaport of Vancouver,
in British Columbia. It ended in November of 1942 at
Halifax, the capital of the peninsula of Nova Scotia. Between these points, which are on opposite sides of the
continent, lay 10,000 miles of icy travel and twenty-eight
months of Arctic loneliness.

Yet, as the little 105-foot Mounted Police schooner *St.
Roch* came into Halifax, rocking in the waves left by
massive transports and battleships, it was ending an historic voyage. When it entered the deep bay, the tiny two-
master had accomplished what no other boat ever had
done before.

The *St. Roch*, piloted and navigated by Mounties, had
sailed from the Pacific to the Atlantic through the Northwest Passage. This was an undertaking which had fired
the imagination of frontiersmen for three centuries.

The Northwest Passage! A route by water from the
Atlantic to the ocean lanes leading to the fabled East, to
the treasures of the Orient! Henry Hudson in his *Half
Moon* had searched for such a route, and so had Cartier
and Cabot and Robert Rogers of Rogers' Rangers.

The route lay along the frosty roof of the North American continent. It was a route plugged by ice and attacked
by gales and blizzards. The famous explorer Amundsen
once had sailed it from the Atlantic to the Pacific. No one

else ever had completed the voyage at all. And now the Mounties were seeking, in their tiny cockle-shell, to find out if the legendary passage could be traveled in the other direction, from the Pacific Ocean to the Atlantic Ocean.

It was a voyage of hardship and desolation, but it started brightly in the blue inlet at Vancouver. The flag of the *St. Roch* flapped in a south wind as a Canadian Pacific switch engine along the shore whistled a saucy farewell.

The *St. Roch* seemed a frail craft in which to brave the crunching jaws of the Polar ice pack. It was only 105 feet long and twenty-five feet wide amidships. The *St. Roch* looked more like a fishing smack than a boat to break open the fabulous Northwest Passage. But it had stout timbers of Douglas fir and the hull was sheathed with Australian "iron bark," the one wood able to resist the terrific pressure of massed ice floes. Its sails were reinforced by a Diesel engine rated at 168 horsepower.

Stuart Taylor Wood, Commissioner of the Royal Canadian Mounted Police, had ordered the *St. Roch* to undertake the dangerous cruise. Commissioner Wood knew the Arctic. Once he had commanded at Herschel Island, far beyond the Circle. By dog sled he had mushed in 60-below weather across the Richardson Mountains from Fort Yukon and Rampart House, a journey which old-timers in the North still talk about.

Still more important, Stuart Taylor Wood, boss of all the Mounties, understood the North by inheritance, too.

He was the son of Zac Wood, the Mounted Police officer who had brought the gold ingots to Skagway in defiance of "Soapy" Smith and his bandit gang.

Commissioner Wood knew exactly what he was doing when he named, as skipper of the *St. Roch*, a tall, blond man born in Norway. This man was Sergeant Henry Larsen.

For nearly twenty years Larsen had helped to keep law and order in the fastnesses extending from Hudson Bay to the Alaskan border. There were few Arctic outposts he had not seen. His assignment placed him aboard a "floating police detachment," which was the way many Mounties referred to the *St. Roch*.

And now at last, with the crown and three gold chevrons of a Sergeant on the sleeve of his uniform, Larsen was attempting the final great exploration possible on the North American continent.

No commissioned officer sailed in the *St. Roch*. Second in command to the 43-year-old Larsen was Corporal M. F. Foster, who had seen nineteen years of service in the force. The rest of the crew consisted of six Constables. The oldest was an immigrant from Wales, W. J. Parry, who at fifty-eight did the cooking and baking. The youngest of the crew was less than half Parry's age—Ed Hadley, 23-year-old radio operator from the Saskatchewan prairies.

Watch them as they go, these eight Canadian Mounties in their bobbing and dipping craft. Destiny travels with them, for this voyage will probably go down in history.

A stiff breeze spanked the *St. Roch* along the fiords of the British Columbia seacoast and into Alaskan waters. At the American Naval Base of Dutch Harbor in the Aleutians, the Mounties stowed aboard stores of food and 2,153 gallons of fuel oil. They ate a chicken dinner with all the trimmings in the messroom of the United States Coast Guard cutter *Shoshone*.

As the crew of the *St. Roch* went down the gangplank, their American hosts commented that the yellow-haired Larsen with his lean Scandinavian face resembled another who had explored the Arctic, Roald Amundsen.

Across the cold water came the friendly farewell: "So long, Mounties. Good luck!"

And the reply: "Good-bye, Yankees. Many thanks!"

In a shroudlike fog the *St. Roch* passed through the Bering Strait between Alaska and Siberia and entered the Arctic Ocean. Immediately the ice pack bared its tusks, and Larsen and his men had a warning of what was to come. The skipper had to weave the *St. Roch* through floes like a football runner in a broken field.

Even in midsummer the chunks of ice were as big as trolley cars. The midnight sun could not melt all the young ice which had formed between these huge bergs. Twice the Mounties had to use blasting powder to free the schooner from the clutch of the pack.

By the time the *St. Roch* reached the lonely R. C. M. P. post at Coppermine, the little boat was badly cracked and beaten. Sergeant Larsen took onto the deck a string of malemutes, for it was evident that soon the early Arctic winter would lock them in the ice. Dog teams would enable them to make patrols where few, if any, white men ever had been before.

They cruised eastward across Coronation Gulf, took on 1,000 gallons of fresh water at Tree River, and poked into the uncharted maze of islands which form the frigid roof of the Western Hemisphere.

And now the northern night was settling down, the night that lasts for half a year. Late in September the ice caught the *St. Roch* in a traplike grip. They were fated to spend the winter in Walker Bay, off the west coast of Victoria Island.

Unloading began immediately. If ice crushed the schooner, they did not want the supplies crushed with her. On those supplies, their lives depended.

The ice tossed and heaved. It squeezed the *St. Roch* like a walnut. Seams were torn apart and water trickled into the forepeak. But the little vessel had sturdy planks and the trickle never became a torrent. The Australian "iron bark" and the Douglas fir from Oregon held staunchly.

The winter was long and dreary. The salvation of the crew of lonely Mounties was the radio panel where Constable Hadley sat at the controls. The Northern Messenger, a special program beamed to the Polar regions from far-off Edmonton, brought them news and tidings of their families and friends at home.

"I wonder," said Corporal Foster, puffing on his briar pipe, "what Arctic explorers did before there were radios?"

"What did Mounted Policemen do?" chimed in Constable Hunt.

Sergeant Larsen had been listening quietly. Now he said: "Most of you know Assistant Commissioner Denny La Nauze. When he was a young man, he was up here more than two years looking for the murderers of Fathers Rouvier and Le Roux. That was before radios. What did he do?"

For ten months the *St. Roch* was cemented in the ice. Would they ever get out? Was there no open water in the summer months at the very top of North America?

But finally, in August, the winds softened and the ice yielded. The long-silent Diesel engines were started. The *St. Roch* moved for the first time in nearly a year. Once the Sergeant had to moor the boat to a towering iceberg so that it would not become entangled in blind leads in the ice pack.

"What happens, Sergeant, if that berg turns over?" asked a Constable.

"We don't think about such things," Larsen answered.

And then, early in September, new ice began to form again. Snow commenced falling. The boat was boxed between two enormous floes, in Pasley Bay. It was maddening. Summer had lasted barely more than a month.

After a voyage of thirty-nine days and less than 400

miles—the result of a year's vigilant effort—the *St. Roch* was once again frozen fast for the winter.

The monotony was now doubly trying. Many months had passed since the Mounties had glimpsed a white settlement. The compass did not work because they were only a few miles from the North Magnetic Pole. Yet even in the never-ending gloom of the Arctic night there was work to be done. This work helped to pass the long hours.

The tall Norwegian-born Sergeant and the 28-year-old Constable P. G. Hunt made one of the stormiest patrols in the history of the Royal Canadian Mounted Police. They were out seventy-one days on the bleak ice pack and traveled 1,160 miles by dog team. Never during that time was the weather warmer than 48 degrees below zero!

Larsen took a census of the Eskimo tribes which had not already been counted, and he and Hunt felt their hearts beat faster when they stumbled onto the wintering place of the old sailing vessel *Victory*. The ship had been abandoned in the ice sheet by Sir John Ross more than a century earlier. They found coils of rope as good as new and just as tough, preserved by temperatures which got down to 75 below zero. The iron of the ancient schooner's engines was being used by the natives for tools and harpoons.

"Let's hope such a fate never overtakes our fine *St. Roch*," said Constable Hunt.

"Aye, aye, Constable," replied the Sergeant feelingly, for the skipper loved his stout little ship.

When, finally, they returned to the *St. Roch*, they found that tragedy had struck in their absence. The cold and desolation had claimed the life of Constable Albert Chartrand. He had patrolled to King William Island to trade for more fur parkas and *mukluks* with the Eskimos. It had been a journey when chilling frost nipped at a man's lungs and he had to be careful not to breathe too deeply. Alcohol froze in the bottle and the touch of metal seared off skin and flesh.

On his return to the boat, Chartrand died of a heart attack. This tragic event took place during one of the worst cold snaps of the dreadful Arctic winter.

Larsen and Hunt harnessed the dogs again and doubled back on their long trek, seeking a wilderness missionary to read the burial service. They buried their comrade beneath a cairn of stones on a rocky islet. Over his grave stood a cross made of lumber from the *St. Roch*. They bowed their heads in sorrow as the aurora borealis crackled in the sky.

The third summer of the voyage was beginning. As the Chinook winds once more softened the ice, the Mounties chipped away at the pack with steel ice chisels. They set off charges with blasting powder. The propellors whirred furiously.

"It's now or never!" shouted the Sergeant.

Again the *St. Roch* shook away the floes. This time the determined Larsen steered due north toward the Pole. He had to get around the rocky Boothia Peninsula. Ice bumped the schooner and broke the Number One cylinder head. Would the motor fail? That could mean their doom. But the grease-covered Corporal Foster, their engineer, managed to keep the Diesels throbbing.

Larsen sighed with relief. He realized they did not have the supplies to spend a third winter locked in the white pincers of the ice pack. Nor, he knew, could the nerves of the men stand such an ordeal.

After a month of the most steady progress they yet had made in the Arctic, the Mounties saw a low-lying coast-line off the starboard beam. They had reached Pond Inlet, the most northerly of all the wilderness outposts of the force. It was even above the North Magnetic Pole. No habitation of white men stood closer to the true North Pole. Pond Inlet had replaced Herschel Island as the most lonely and far-flung of any Mounted Police detachment. Its two isolated Constables puffed their pipes and trained their bushy-haired sled dogs within hailing distance of the point where every horizon faces south.

And now the *St. Roch* weighed anchor and ran down the coast of Baffinland, dodging icebergs bigger than ocean liners. Off the shore of Labrador they groped through pea-soup fog, but at last put the frigid seas behind them as they rounded Newfoundland. When they swung in at Halifax harbor, they had voyaged 10,000 miles and been away from civilization for almost two and a half years.

It was a journey which demonstrated many things. It showed that the Northwest Passage could be navigated from the Pacific to the Atlantic. If the *St. Roch*, with its wooden planks, could slip across the Hemisphere, then steel ice-breakers, fitted with the turbines of Victory Ships, might possibly open a new route from ocean to ocean.

In 1944 Henry Larsen had orders to get his hardy *St. Roch* back to British Columbia. Two routes were possible. He could swing south, tasting tropical seas, and sail through the Panama Canal. Or, he could brave the Northwest Passage again.

The North was in the skipper's blood. "I'll take the high road," said the Mounted Police Sergeant.

This time everything broke right for the floating detachment of Mounties. Where before the ice had snatched at the *St. Roch* with a viselike grip, open leads of clear water now appeared. Eighty-six days after sailing out of Halifax harbor, the *St. Roch* was cruising beneath the Lions' Gate Bridge into the wide bay at Vancouver.

Banners and pennants flew proudly from the masts of the tiny schooner. Its decks were scoured. The brass and other metalwork gleamed like mirrors. No other ship ever had sailed through the Northwest Passage so speedily. No other ship ever had sailed the Northwest Passage from west to east. No other ship ever had sailed the Northwest Passage in both directions.

And Henry A. Larsen, Norwegian-born Sergeant of the Royal Canadian Mounted Police, had become the most successful skipper in the history of that ocean corridor which men had sought to conquer for more than 300 years.

But Henry Larsen was not to remain a Sergeant for long. Today he is Inspector Henry A. Larsen, and he commands "G" Division of the Mounted. This is the division with the longest law-enforcement arm in the world. It reaches out from Ottawa and patrols the greatest wilderness left on our continent—the Yukon and Northwest Territories.

10

The Streamlined Mounties of Today

AT THE END OF A BRITISH COLUMBIA INLET WITH GRANITE walls, the body of a salmon fisherman of the Tshimshean Indian Tribe has been found, a bullet hole between the eyes. The dead man's fish nets slosh beside him in the cold green tide.

From Port Alberni, on wooded Vancouver Island, a sleek 80-foot motor launch puts out through the choppy waters of the North Pacific. The throbbing of its motors echoes against the steep shoreline. Aboard *Motor Launch 16* are three young men in oil-stained coveralls. They travel by darkness and by light to reach the scene of the murdre.

Into a footprint near the body, they pour plaster to get a mold of the mark left behind by a possible suspect. One of the young men takes pictures of the Indian's body with a bright new camera. He studies a hair in the cuff of the blazer worn by the murdered man. He puts the hair between glass slides.

"Sergeant Solly in the crime lab will want to look at this," he mutters, half to himself.

From a splintered log on the beach, another man of the launch's crew pries a dented bullet. He peers at it through a thick lens, like the lens used by watchmakers. In a note-book he scribbles that the bullet probably is of .303 caliber. Then he packs the bullet in cotton. It could lead them to the murderer.

The third young sailor sits in the cabin of *M. L. 16* flashing a message by radio to Superintendent Archer's headquarters in Vancouver, 200 miles off to the south. Beneath the greasy coveralls worn by the crew of the glistening launch bulge shoulder bars with the magic letters R. C. M. P.

The Mounties of today have gone modern. They use speedboats, airplanes, and crime-detection laboratories to go about their business. They are streamlined, mechanized, and motorized.

We think of the Mounties astride galloping steeds, but actually they ride fewer horses now than does the police department of New York City! The Mounties own 151 saddle horses, as compared with the 278 horses which carry New York's traffic policemen.

You may see Mounties in their thrilling "Musical Ride" at an exhibition in the United States. You may see a red-coated Constable on a proud stallion, guarding the Peace Tower in Ottawa, where the Canadian Parliament sits in session.

This is because all members of the force learn to handle a horse. They must be prepared for any emergency. Wilderness duty could fall to each of them. In addition, it is good discipline to ride in tricky formations.

A red-coated Constable guards the Peace Tower at Ottawa.

But an up-to-date Mountie is mounted not back of a flying mane but behind an eight-cylinder engine. He drives a car. This is one of the first things he must learn to do properly when he joins the force.

"Once we needed stablemen, dog-mushers, veterinarians, cowboys, and ring-masters," said Inspector Edward H. Stevenson, a 6-foot 4-inch Mountie who is in charge of training in British Columbia. "In this modern age our needs run more to mechanics, radio operators, airplane pilots, and skilled chemists and photographers."

I saw this gradual change in the famous police organization when I was stationed in Canada's picturesque North Country during World War II.

At Whitehorse, from which stern-wheeled river boats start down the Yukon, the detachment consisted of four Mounties. Yukon Territory headquarters were 300 miles away in the quiet old gold-rush settlement of Dawson, where fourteen men were on duty. They had little need for automobiles. No road led far out of Dawson.

Slowly, the highway to Alaska was hacked out of the dense spruce forests. At last it reached Whitehorse, where bulldozers also cleared a mile-long airplane runway. Instead of frozen fish for sled dogs, the Mounties now had to order high-octane motor fuel for cars which would be expected to travel when the temperature went down to 65 below zero.

Today only four Mounties are left at Dawson City.

Whitehorse, the new headquarters for the Yukon Territory, has a strength of seventeen. Last year these men patrolled 169,000 miles on the Alaska Highway by car. Mounties who once fought their way through this wild realm on Cree hunting snowshoes now purr along behind the steering wheels of Fords, Pontiacs, and Chevrolets.

Sergeant Barry Allen said to me, "The North is changing, and we of the Mounted Police are changing with it. We are using more scientific and mechanical equipment with every passing year."

On the Alaska Highway, the careless motorist may hear a warning siren at his back. He comes to a nervous halt. Behind him is a patrol car, painted black and white. Blinker lights are on the roof. A radio telephone hangs from the dashboard, although the car may be so far from a detachment that the radio cannot be used. The front fender carries the megaphone of a loudspeaker, just like any police car in the big city.

A sturdy Constable strolls over the gravel road to the tourist's automobile and asks in a polite voice, "May I see your driver's license, please?"

The Constable seems friendly, but there is no doubt that he means business. Nor is there any mistaking the organization which he represents.

His badges and buttons are plain for all to see. He wears a tunic of dark brown and not the brilliant scarlet, which is reserved for such tourist centers as Banff and Jasper National Parks. Looped over the Constable's shoulder is a Sam Brown belt; a revolver and leather ammunition case are at his waist.

Perhaps more than any other police organization in the world, the Mounties combine the old and the new. One Constable may be driving a bright new Ford coupe over the Alaska Highway. At the same time another Constable of "G" Division may be mushing alone through the Northwest Territories behind a string of fourteen yipping Husky sled dogs. In the very year that Mounties patrolled 105,000 miles in the North by airplane, they also journeyed 49,000 miles by dog sled.

Although the Mounties own a total of 1,219 motor vehicles, they also rely on 235 bushy sled dogs to help them patrol the icy reaches of the Arctic.

But the Mounties use motors and engines wherever they can. They realize that criminals have access to these inventions, and the force must keep pace.

The Aviation Section of the Mounted Police is staffed mainly by combat fliers with experience in the Royal Canadian Air Force. They pilot a dozen planes on errands of mercy and justice into the lonely Canadian "bush."

The Mounties travel by boat as well as by plane. Canada is a country of lakes and rivers and ocean fiords, and so the Marine Division is a small navy in itself. It has eighty-six boats and 212 officers and enlisted men. In World War II some of these boats sailed the North Atlantic, and many of the Mountie sailors lost their lives to keep the supplies going to Britain.

A few of the boats of the Marine Division are mere outboard skiffs or launches. Yet others are 112-foot cutters and converted corvettes. Some of the Bangor-class minesweepers measure 162 feet from bow to stern. This is nearly the size of a destroyer.

The Mounted Police patrol ship *Irvine*, named for an officer who served during Fort Whoop-Up days, once ventured far out toward Greenland to rescue the crew of the sinking Dutch freighter *Marleen*. This ship was thought to be headed for Davy Jones' Locker at the bottom of the ocean, but the sea-going Mounties brought it safely to harbor.

In port, a Mountie Staff Sergeant set free the frozen anchor of the Dutch steamer by wrapping mattresses around the ice-coated chain. Then he drenched the mattresses with kerosene and put them on fire. They blazed merrily. Soon the *Marleen* was securely anchored to the floor of the harbor.

Every danger to the safety and welfare of the Canadian nation draws the attention of the Mounties.

At one time the Spanish government's consul in Montreal was suspected of being in league with a gang of smugglers. To solve the case, Sergeant C. C. Brown of the Mounted Police went to work on it for two years.

Sergeant Brown crossed the ocean to Barcelona, in Spain. There he carefully arranged for a fake series of illegal shipments into Canada. These trapped the crafty Don Miguel Malaguer y Salvador. They also sent to trial some dishonest members of the Canadian Customs Ser-vice, who were the Spaniard's partners.

Of course, on this daring mission to a distant land, Sergeant Brown wore only civilian clothes. His dashing uniform was left at home in the closet and he was known as plain "Mr. Robino."

Mounties played the leading part in cracking a Soviet spy ring, which was scheming to deliver Canada's military secrets to the Russians. The man who wrecked this dangerous plot was an R. C. M. P. Inspector named John Leopold, who had sailed to Canada originally as a young immigrant from Bohemia in Central Europe.

To become a Mountie, an immigrant first must take out British or Canadian citizenship. A new member entering the force cannot be younger than eighteen or older than thirty. He must not be shorter than 5 feet 8 inches in height, and he cannot weigh more than 210 pounds. His chest has to measure at least thirty-five inches before he puffs it up with a deep breath. And he must have gone through at least the eighth grade in school.

Somebody once asked several Mountie recruits what they did. And they sang back in chorus:

"You work, you work, you work!"

Six months of training are required to produce a Mountie. The two main instruction centers have been Rockcliffe Barracks near Ottawa and the Western Training Depot in Regina, on the Saskatchewan prairies. Another training post recently was set up at Fairmont Barracks in Van-

couver. Fairmont offers "refresher" courses for men who
have been at bleak detachments in the wilds.

Neither a dunce nor a weakling can be a Mountie. Box-
ing, wrestling, horsemanship, swimming, jiu-jitsu—these
are some of the physical routines a Mountie must master.
He also must learn to punch a typewriter at the rate of
thirty words a minute or better.

"We want no smudgy chicken-track reports on important cases coming out of the North," said Inspector
Stevenson, one of the training instructors.

The Mountie of old had to be able to harness sled dogs
and tie a diamond-hitch on the load carried by a pack-
horse. The Mountie of today often must be able to perform these tasks and many others, too.

He must be able to read fingerprints. He has to operate
a camera. He must know ballistics, which means picking
out the gun that fired a certain bullet. He studies toxicology, or the science of poisons, for these are commonly
used by murderers. And he learns about history, politics,
and government.

Strict military discipline governs Mounties in training.
"Lights out" is sounded by a bugle at 10:45 at night.
There are many inspections, with all kit from Stetson
hats to lanyards and face towels displayed on iron cots in
apple-pie order. The new Mounties hurry from classrooms
to revolver practice and back again. Stables also must be
cleaned, lawns mowed, and mess halls painted.

Why this strenuous schooling for men who will enforce

Canada's law? When I was in Ottawa for conferences regarding the route of the Alaska Highway, I asked this question of Commissioner Stuart Taylor Wood, who retired not long ago. Before retirement, he had been the top-ranking Mountie of them all.

"Being a member of the R. C. M. P. is more than being an ordinary policeman," replied the Commissioner. "The Mounted Police have many posts where one man may have great responsibility. He must make decisions quickly and on his own. He may be far from his commanding officer. He must have a lot of different skills. He migh have to be a doctor one minute and a cook the next.

"And he must have a sense of tradition. That is why he never wears a red tunic until graduation day at Rockcliffe or Regina. He may not wear the red tunic very often again, but it has for him rich meaning. It helps make him aware of the great deeds done by the force in the past."

Wood was succeeded as boss Mountie by 48-year-old Leonard H. Nicholson, who has served in the force since he was nineteen. Nicholson, a sturdy graying man, is a crack rifle shot.

This new Commissioner of the Mounties was Provost Marshal of the Canadian Army overseas during World War II. The Provost Marshal has charge of all military policemen. These are the troops who keep order in an army. Many Mounties served as military policemen in the front lines in every war in which Canada has fought.

As the Number One Mountie in all of Canada, Commissioner Nicholson wears on his shoulders the same insignia as a Brigadier General in the Canadian Army. His annual pay is $15,000.

Would you like to know the salaries that other Mounties are paid? The Deputy Commissioner receives $10,000 a year, each of the nine Assistant Commissioners $7,500, a Superintendent $6,700, an Inspector $6,000, a Staff Sergeant $3,900, a Sergeant $3,600, a Corporal $3,300 and a beginning first-class Constable $2,520.

A member of the force may retire with a pension at the end of twenty years of service. Along the Alaska Highway and down the broad Mackenzie River, I have talked with grizzled traders and trappers who receive a check every month from the Ministry of Justice. The money comes as a reward for faithful service in the Mounted Police. These men were ex-Mounties who could not stay away from the North.

Near Fort Nelson an ex-Corporal said to me, "After I got my pension I figured I would have a big time in Winnipeg or Toronto. But the North was in my blood. I decided that I'd have to spend the rest of my life up where I did my duty as a Mounted Policeman."

And the white-haired man went back to his homesteading and trapping and timber-cutting.

Like Commissioner Nicholson, many modern Mounties are expert shots with a rifle or pistol. But like *Stamix*

Otokon and other famous Mounties of the past, they shoot only rarely in the course of their duties.

Inspector R. A. S. MacNeil, who supervises Mounted Police public relations at Ottawa, has given this explanation of that policy:

"Shooting is discouraged as much as possible. Our men are expected to use no more force than is really necessary when making an arrest. If shooting is required for the safety of the public—if a man commits murder and then runs—then the Mounted Police shoot to halt rather than to kill."

The Mounties are proud that they seldom have to eye a man along their pistol barrels. In the frontier town of Prince George, where brawny lumberjacks frequently come for a wild weekend, I had coffee and hotcakes with a rangy Constable. He had broken his right hand on stubborn jaws three times in less than two years.

"But I never threatened a drunk or a bully with a gun," the Mountie assured me. "That would simply build up a bully. It would make him more anxious to pick on people who couldn't fight back. I'd trust my fist rather than my gun to take the steam out of a bully, who was making life miserable for folks smaller and weaker than himself."

The commanding officer of the Mounties in Prince George, on the headwaters of the mighty Fraser River, was a tall, slender man named Syd Batty. He had served overseas during nearly all of World War II. As a young Constable of the Mounted Police in Saskatchewan, he had chased a bank robber six miles on foot, over hill and down dale.

"I was in full uniform and kit, and the robber had on tennis shoes and a thin sweater," said Inspector Batty. "But I made up my mind I wouldn't shoot him. I didn't want to risk taking his life. I finally caught him when he collapsed on the ground from the strain of running so far and so fast."

Does the fact that the Mounties are not trigger-happy ever endanger the lives of these brave men who wear *Maintiens le Droit* on their buttons?

In Montreal in 1950 a bank holdup man killed an unarmed Mountie Constable, who grappled him with bare hands on the street. The name of the valiant Mountie was Alexander Gamman.

Following the murder, grim men flung a barricade of sharp eyes and pointed questions all the way across the country. Five months later Constable Gamman's slayer felt handcuffs on his wrists near Big Beaver, Saskatchewan. Within another five months he had dropped through a gallows trap door. Never again would he be able to take another life.

Streamlined equipment helps the Mounted Police. Yet some members of the modern force believe this equipment is not always better than the old way of doing things.

C. E. Rivett-Carnac, a massive man of fifty, is Assistant

Commissioner in command of the 855 Mounties on duty in British Columbia. He thinks the airplane in the North should be given only limited use, if a trooper is to patrol his district efficiently.

"You've got to know the trappers and the woodsmen and the Indians personally," said Rivett-Carnac, who is descended from a British family of royal heritage. "Otherwise you never will really get to the bottom of the crimes and troubles in which they may be involved.

"When I was stationed at Aklavik on the Arctic Ocean," he continued, "I flew one way on patrol but I traveled by

snowshoes and dog team in the other direction. I bunked with the lonely people of the wilderness and thus got to know them. You've got to break bread with a man to understand what makes him tick. It was maddening, though, to be buzzed by a bush pilot and to realize he would be warm and cozy in town in four hours, while I wouldn't get there on snowshoes for four weeks!"

Rivett-Carnac is typical of adventurers from England, whose love of excitement originally attracted them to the Mounted Police. Once he fought in the French Army and later he drove elephants in the teak forests of India.

"But being a Mountie in the Arctic was the greatest experience of all," said the Assistant Commissioner. "I felt I really amounted to something. I was game warden, policeman, and port director for an area about the size of Merry Old England itself."

Few Americans really understand the type of authority which the Mounted Police have in Canada. The jurisdiction of Rivett-Carnac in British Columbia is an example.

Everywhere in Canada the Mounties enforce Federal laws, which are passed by the Parliament at Ottawa. These laws apply to immigration, smuggling, narcotics, sabotage, spying, and other national problems. Rivett-Carnac's principal aide is Superintendent George J. Archer in Vancouver. He directs many plain-clothes men whose duty it is to keep undesirable aliens, illegal drugs, and forbidden goods from entering Canada's greatest seaport on the Pacific Ocean.

Besides this Federal authority all over Canada, the Mounties act as provincial police in eight provinces. These provinces are Prince Edward Island, Nova Scotia, Newfoundland, New Brunswick, Manitoba, Saskatchewan, Alberta, and British Columbia.

The Legislature of any province may contract with the Canadian government "for the services of the Royal Canadian Mounted Police to enforce the provincial statutes and criminal code within the boundaries of that province." This gives the Mounties wider powers than State Police in the United States. Only two Canadian provinces, Ontario and Quebec, have not taken advantage of this arrangement.

The province pays the national Ministry of Justice $1,400 for each Mountie assigned to duty. The R. C. M. P. in 1951 took over both the Provincial Force of British Columbia and the Newfoundland Rangers. Members of the two disbanded organizations who could qualify were enlisted as Mounties.

I have talked with Premier Ernest C. Manning of Alberta about this plan. "It is thrifty for the province and it is popular," he told me. "Then too, it removes law-enforcement from politics."

"K" Division of the Mounted, for example, includes all of Alberta, an area nearly the size of Texas. It is commanded by a crisp, terse officer named Alan Thomas Belcher. He rose in the ranks after having been a Constable at isolated Arctic outposts. His father was the determined

Inspector Bobby Belcher who built the post at the top of bleak Chilkoot Pass.

The North runs strongly in the veins of Assistant Commissioner Belcher; his great-grandfather sailed from England into the ice pack and helped to map some of the islands between Hudson's Bay and the North Pole.

One day I watched Belcher, followed by his Sergeant-Major, inspect the automobile fleet of "K" Division. Then he said to me:

"It's not as romantic as when the cavalry column was lined up on frisky horses and the band played *Maple Leaf Forever*. But automobiles help make the best use of our limited manpower, and we have to keep up with the twentieth century in which we live."

All Mountie recruits still must be single men. But once a Constable has served his five-year hitch and gets married, his wife can go with him, no matter how lonely the outpost.

Many of the wilderness detachments consist of a house divided equally between living quarters and a police office. When the Mountie is away on patrol, his wife may operate the radio which keeps in touch with a distant headquarters. In the Alberta "bush" north of Edmonton, I met a pretty young woman who fed one holdup man in a boxlike cell, while her husband roamed mossy swamps in search of the man's partner.

When the Constable, six-feet five-inches tall, came back with the other criminal, I asked him if he had been worried about the safety of his wife. "No," he answered. "She's the best jailer, radio operator, car driver, and general handy person our force could have!"

Although the modern Mounties are stern in dealing with the guilty, they take pride in parceling out mercy to the innocent.

The treasurer of a Canadian city was charged with stealing after a flash fire had burned all the money in his chambers. High officials thought that he had made off with the funds, which probably were in a secret hiding place somewhere. They suspected he had set the fire himself to cover up the theft.

But the man had a good reputation and the Mounties believed the accusation to be false. The crime-detection laboratory at Rockcliffe Barracks carefully sifted through heaps of ashes from the fire. Out of the ashes, the Mounties created anew nearly every piece of paper money which had been in the city treasurer's office at the time of the fire.

Thus it was proved that the man had not taken the money after all. He had a chance to return to his position of public trust. Gratefully, he thanked the Mounties with tears in his eyes.

This was not as glamorous a deed as tracking killers in the frozen wastes. But it was important to upholding the right in Canada, and that was what counted with the Mounties.

Anything which succeeds is frequently copied. Alaska,

that majestic Northern realm owned by the United States, now is setting up a Territorial Police Corps which will be patterned after the Mounties. As these words are written, the Alaska legislature in Juneau has passed a bill calling for policemen who will operate just as the Mounties do in Canada. "I hope this will enable us," said the Governor of Alaska, "to cut down Alaska's high crime rate and secure the obedience to law and order which the Mounted Police maintain across the border in British Columbia and the Yukon Territory."

11

Some Mounties Who Are Friends of Mine

JOHN MACDOUGALL PIPER IS THIRTEEN YEARS OLD. HIS
sister's name is Elizabeth Susan Piper. She was born nine
years ago. Both these children go to school in the little
Canadian city of Chilliwack.

Chilliwack lies in the center of the beautiful Fraser
River Valley, where green dairy pastures form a checker-
board with the darker green of groves of fir trees. Chilliwack is in British Columbia, twenty-five miles from the
boundary which separates that province from the state of
Washington.

John and his sister are often the envy of the other children, because their father is a Mountie. He wears the
three handsome gold chevrons of a Sergeant on his sleeve.
His name is John Fraser Piper and he is forty-three years
old. He has been a Mountie since he was only twenty-one.
At present Sergeant John Piper is the principal non-
commissioned officer for a huge area which includes
eighteen Mounted Police posts.

My wife and I have been guests of the Piper family in
their little pink stucco house, bordered by gladiolas and
pansies. The mother of John MacDougall and Susan is
dark-haired Aimee Piper. Her rich chocolate cake is fa-

mous all over Chilliwack. Before we returned to the United States, my wife made sure that she had the recipe for this wonderful cake in her purse.

Aimee and her husband had a real Mounted Police romance before they were married.

In 1934 John Fraser Piper, then a new Constable in the force, was "posted" for duty in the majestic Yukon Territory. This was welcome news to him because his own father had been the Corporal Storm Piper who helped to solve the killing of poor Leon Bouthillette during the Klondike gold rush. Now he was to serve in the very wilderness where his father had helped to make history!

On the old river steamer *Kaska*, bound down the Yukon through Five-Finger Rapids, Constable Piper met a pretty nurse who was going to Dawson to work in a hospital.

Piper and the nurse fell in love, but a Mountie has to be in the force at least five years before he can take a bride. As a result, Aimee and John had a long engagement period.

"My bridal veil and wedding dress became awfully out of date," laughed Aimee.

But at last the five years were up, and Constable Piper had the permission of his commanding officer to get married.

And now we were in the pleasant home of this couple who had had a typical Mounted Police courtship in the wild and icy North Country! We found the Pipers just like any other normal, healthy family.

That night when Sergeant Piper came home from post headquarters for dinner, he took off his brown tunic with

Sergeant Piper with John, Jr., and Elizabeth Susan.

its brass buttons and hung it in the closet. Then he put on a smoking jacket with velvet collar and cuffs, to wear at the table. It made a strange contrast with his yellow-striped blue breeches.

Then Aimee Piper served fried chicken with creamy country gravy, and the father and the two children could hardly wait for full plates of food. However, the Mountie first said a short blessing over the meal, while all of us at the table sat with bowed heads.

Sergeant Piper takes part in the community life of Chilliwack, like any other good citizen. He has a Sunday School class in the United Church of Canada. His wife Aimee teaches the "baby" Sunday School group. This consists of children in the kindergarten ages. The first Sunday that John Piper had his class, the boys went home gasping:

"Gee, Pop, guess who's our Sunday School teacher! A real live Mountie, sure enough!"

Sergeant John Piper also has been the Cub Scoutmaster in several towns where he has been stationed. In fact, he founded a series of Cub Scout Troops, as part of the Mountie program for boys.

Every Mountie has a regimental number. He keeps the same number throughout his years of service in the force. It never goes to another man. Sergeant John Piper's number is 11929. One other number is fixed in his memory. It is that held by his father when he was a red-coated trooper in the Arctic: Regimental No. 2349.

John MacDougall and Elizabeth Susan frequently ask

169

their father for stories about the great days when he himself was on duty in the North. They never tire of these tales. Nor do the other children in Chilliwack.

Four times a year the *R. C. M. P. Quarterly* arrives by mail in the Piper household. This is a magazine published at the national headquarters of the Mounted Police in Ottawa. It tells about the activities of members of the force and of hard cases solved by the Mounties. When the *Quertarly* comes, the Piper children seek a seat by the hearth fire while their father reads to them about the famous force of which he is a member.

And, of course, John MacDougall and Elizabeth Susan are particularly proud on the Queen's Birthday, Dominion Day, and other Canadian holidays. On such occasions their father wears his scarlet jacket, with the brilliant facings and decorations of gold and blue.

Mounties never know when they will be transferred. Canada is one of the world's largest countries and there are at least 600 detachments where a trooper can be stationed. But if Sergeant Piper goes somewhere else, his children will find new playmates and new friends. Naturally, John MacDougall and his sister hope they can continue to be near their grandfather, ex-Corporal Piper, who lives in British Columbia and who has drawn a pension from the force for nearly thirty-five years.

Because the Mounties are so effective a police force, many of us think of the individual members as supermen.

After having met members of the force like Sergeant Piper and others, I realized that this is not so. They are flesh-and-blood people, just like anybody else.

After three years of residence and many travels in Canada, I number a host of friends in the Mounted Police. Their names often come to mind. I recall warm-hearted, friendly men with real understanding of other people.

I remember Commissioner Wood, an officer of stern visage with iron-gray hair. Yet his face relaxed and he thumbed a book of history fondly, when he talked of his father's deeds in the Klondike. And he said he was proud that the Mounted never tried to get "confessions" from people by force or cruelty. One of Commissioner Wood's sons lost his life in the Royal Canadian Mounted Police while on duty with "K" Division in Alberta. Another son was killed in the Royal Canadian Air Force during World War II.

And now the ex-Commissioner, in retirement, lives on the Mounted Police Ranch near Maple Creek, Saskatchewan. There he raises remounts for the celebrated "Musical Ride," when the Mounties in dashing crimson ride prancing steeds at exhibitions and horse shows in the United States.

I look back with fond memories upon the pleasant picnic which my wife and I had with Inspector Syd Batty and his family in a pine forest near Prince George. The Inspector wore flannel slacks and a sport shirt. He brought along an indoor baseball to play "catch." Like any other husband and father, he smiled affectionately at his witty wife Ann and their frisky daughter, eight-year-old Gay.

As we ate potato salad and cold roast beef, I thought to myself that this was just another picnic with a fine, friendly Canadian family. No one would have known that the man beside us was the noted Inspector Batty, who commanded Mountie patrols all the way from the Nechako River to the Yukon line.

Many images like this thread through my mind. The Mounties may be supermen when they are on the trail of a criminal. But otherwise they are no different from other husbands and fathers and friends.

Sergeant John Piper and his wife, for example, have taken out savings policies for their two children. These are paid with the Family Allowances money that comes from the Canadian government to Mrs. Piper each month. The parents hope that this security will help their son to be a Mountie and the daughter to be a nurse, copying the careers of their parents.

It has seemed to me that almost every time I meet a Mountie on duty, he says he is the son of a man who served before him with the gleaming initials "RCMP" on his blue shoulder straps. Denny La Nauze, John Piper, Alan Belcher of "K" Division, ex-Commissioner Wood— all these members of the force referred to themselves as coming from "Mounted Police families."

And the wives of Mounties are exceedingly human, too. I still can hear Bella La Nauze telling me how she had to barricade the bungalow door against a great grizzly bear weighing nearly half a ton, while her husband was stationed in the Canadian Rockies, near Banff. I also remember Ann Batty describing the struggle of a girl from a quiet house in the English countryside to share the rugged life of her Mountie husband on the muskeg at Yellowknife, in the Northwest Territories.

Yet one memory stands out above all others.

When I went north a few summers ago, Denny La Nauze told me to look up some of his old pals along the vast Mackenzie River system. The man who captured Sinnisiak and Uluksak was retired, after rising to be Assistant Commissioner of the force.

How would I be received? After all, a Mountie officer must have had to arrest many people during thirty-five years on the force!

I walked into a boat yard on the Athabaska River near Fort McMurray. Dark Chipewyan Indians with braided hair were building boats. They had never heard of me. They did not know who I was or where I was from, but the instant I mentioned the name of Denny La Nauze, they dropped their draw-knives and axes. They gathered around me and shook my hand. How long since I had seen La Nauze? If I was a friend of La Nauze, I was a friend of theirs!

Granny McDermott, eighty years old, came running from a nearby house. "They say no one ever loves a policeman, but we all loved Denny La Nauze," said this elderly woman with silvery hair and lined, brown face.

"La Nauze knew more than all the rest of us put together, but he never interrupted a conversation. He heard an Indian stevedore right through to the end." This was told me by the skipper of a Diesel tug, which was barging pitchblende for the atomic bomb from Port Radium.

It was like this all through the realm of the Mackenzie, Canada's greatest river.

At last I saw Denny La Nauze himself again. By what standard had he lived to occupy so firm a place in the hearts of the wilderness folk? In the orange glow of the fireplace, memories lighted up the face of this man who had been a Mountie for so long.

"My mother, who brought me up in Ireland," he said, "had faith in each human spirit. Something she told me I never forgot, no matter where I was."

The famous old Mountie continued:

" 'Denny,' said my mother to me, 'always remember that all people make mistakes. You can be very sure of yourself, but never refuse to listen. The other fellow may be right!' "

Silence held us at the hearth fire. I looked at the Mountie who had spent twenty-eight months in the barren lands, tracking down the slayers of Fathers Rouvier and Le Roux. His eyes were misty. He brushed them with a big white linen handkerchief.

And so I knew that Mounties were very human, just like the rest of us.

When the wire came telling me that Denny La Nauze had died, I put it down and thought hard of the scarlet police and their role in the vast land that we know as Canada. And I could hear the tears of the wilderness folks dropping, from Peace River Crossing to the Polar Sea.

Index

Alaska, crime, 83–84, 87–89, 164
Alaska Highway, 10, 13, 19, 28–31, 149–51, 155; dedication 28–31
Alberni (port), 145; *map*, 8
Alberta, Canada, 64, 161, 162
Albert (Mount), 7; *map*, 8
Aleutian Islands, 137
Allen, Barry, ix, 14, 150
Allen, Inspector, 56, 78
Almighty Voice (outlaw), 67, 78
Amundsen, Roald, 134, 137
Applewhaite, E. T., x
Archer, George J., ix, 146, 160
Arden, D'Arcy, 117, 119
Assiniboine Indians, 33–34
Baltimore, Maryland, murders, 15
Bank robbery, 158
Batty, Syd, 157–58, 172–73
Belcher, Alan Thomas, ix, 161–62, 173
Belcher, Bobby, 81, 162
Beaudoin, Guy, 91–93
Bi-lingualism, 10, 37
Blackfoot nation, 53, 57, 59, 60
Blackstone River Divide, 98, 101
Bonanza Creek, 79, 91
Bond (whisky trader), 45–49
Bonnet Plume (watershed), 96
Bouthillette, Leon, 91–94
British Columbia, 6, 63–64, 74, 145, 161
Brown, C. C., 152–53
Bruce, Wyndham V., 124, 128
Bully, taking the steam out of a, 157

Burns, Jack, 91, 93
Bush, Kenneth B., x
Button Chief, 53
Calgary, Alberta, 64; *map*, 8
Campbell, J. Hugh, x
Camsell, Charles, ix
Canada, 3–7, 10–11; area, 133, 170; boundary, 69–70; confederation, 34; Federal authority, 160–61; holidays, 170; knowledge about, 133; safety, 152
Canadian Pacific Railway, 61–78
Carmack (white man), 79
Carter, Sam, 99, 101, 102, 104, 107–08
Caulkin, Sergeant-Major, 130
Chartrand, Albert, 141
Cheechakos (tenderfeet), 79–80, 82, 90
Children, 21–22
Chilkat Indians, 88–89
Chilkoot Pass, 79–81, 83, 87, 92; *map*, 8
Chilliwack, British Columbia, 165–66, 169, 170
Chinook (winds), 83, 119, 141
Chipewyan Indians, 22–23, 174
Colebrook, Charles, 67, 78
Constantin, Alphonse, 91
Continental Limited (train), 3–5
Coppermine (post), 137; *map*, 8
Coppermine (river), 110, 112, 119, 121
Coronation Gulf, 110, 138; *map*, 8
Craigellachie (station), 70, 78; *map*, 8
Cree Indians, 16–17, 54, 65–67

Crime-detection laboratories, 146, 163
Crime rate, 15
Cronkhite, H. H., ix, 28
Crowfoot (leader), 59, 65, 70, 73
Crozier, Inspector, 46
Custer, General George A., 54–55, 57
Cypress Hills, 33, 53
Dawson City, 79, 82, 92–93, 95, 98,
    101–02, 149; *map*, 8
De Lisle, Cliff, 24–25
Dempster, Corporal, 109
Denny, Cecil, 50
Dickens, Francis J., 87
Duck Lake detachment, 67–69
Dufferin (camp), Manitoba, 38–42, 50
Dunn, William, 74
Dutch Harbor (Naval Base), 137
Eagle Tail (chief), 58–59
Edmonton, Alberta, 115, 126, 162;
    map, 8
Esau (Indian), 99, 101
Eskimo people, 19, 22, 23, 110, 130,
    133, 140
Fairbanks, Alaska, 10; *map*, 8
Fairmont Barracks, 153–54
Family Allowances, 21–22, 173
Fargo, North Dakota, 38; *map*, 9
Fingerprints, 154
Finnie, Richard, ix
Fire water. *See* Whisky
Fitzgerald, Francis J., 97–99, 101,
    102, 103, 104, 107, 108, 109
Fleming, George, ix
Forrest, Constable, 98–99, 101, 102
Fort Whoop-Up, 32, 34, 41, 45, 52
Forty-Mile, 109; *map*, 8
Foster, M. F., 136, 139, 142
Fournier (murderer), 93–95
Franklin, Sir John, 124
Frapance, Father, 114, 117, 119, 120,
    121
Fraser River, 157
French, George A., 38, 43, 130–33
Frostbite, 28, 30
Fury, Sergeant, 61, 62, 78
Gallant, Father Edgar, 80–81

Gamblers, 82
Gamman, Alexander, 158
Gatling guns, 69
Gold Rush, 79–95
Grand Prairie, *map*, 8
Grasshoppers, 42
Great Bear Lake, 7, 118, 119
Grennan, William, ix
Guilty (the), 163
Hadley, Ed, 136, 138
Halbrite, Saskatchewan, 75
Halifax, Nova Scotia, *map*, 9; *Saint
    Roch*, voyages, 134, 142, 144
Hann, George T., ix
Hart River, 96
Helena, Montana, 45, 50–52; *map*, 8
Henry rifles, 45
Herschel Island, 124, 126, 135, 142;
    map, 8
Homesteading, 34, 37
Horse(s), 42, 146, 172
Horsemanship, 154
House of Commons, 68
Howard, Joseph Kinsey, x
Hudson's Bay Company, 20
Hunt, Constable P. G., 140, 141
Hunter, Alec, x
Huron Indians, 3
Huskies, 23, 24, 100, 121, 151
"Idaho Kid, " 74–76
Ilavernik, Constable, 117–18, 120, 121,
    122, 124, 125, 127, 128
Immigration, 153, 160
Indian(s): courage, 54; fear, 54;
    friends, 51, 59; hunting grounds, 54;
    Mounties, 70; railroad, 65–67; sym-
    bols, 37; whisky, 32–33, 45–47, 52–
    53, 59; witchcraft, 90; women, 51–52
Indian country, possessing liquor in,
    49
Indian Treaty Day, 21, 58, 60
Inspections, 154
Instruction centers, 153–55
Irvine (patrol ship), 152
James, Jesse, 73
Jiu-jitsu, 154

Index

Jomini, Harry J., ix
Joseph (chief), 54
Kamloops, British Columbia, 73–74
Kanata. See Canada
Kaska (steamer), 166
Keenleyside, Dr. Hugh L., ix
Kicking Horse Pass, 69
Kice-picim, 126
King William Island, 141
Kinney, George, 99, 107, 109
Kipling, Rudyard, 97
Klondike Gold Rush, 79–95
Kluane Lake, 29
Klukwan (village), 89–90
Kodik (boy), torturing, 89–90
Kogloktogmiuts, 113, 118, 122-23, 125, 126, 127
LaBelle (murderer), 93–95
Labrador, 142
Lambert (cape), 124; *map*, 8
La Nauze, Charles Deering, ix, 115–28, 129, 173–75
Land companies, 54
Larsen, Henry A., ix, 136–44
Launches, 152
Law, protection of, 55
Leeson, Constable, 89, 90
Leopold, John, 153
Le Roux, George (priest), 110–14, 117–19, 126
Lethbridge, Alberta, 32; *map*, 8
Lett, Constable, 75–76, 78
Lewis and Clark Expedition, 10
Liard (river), 115
Little Wind River, 96, 101, 102
Liquor traffic, 64
"Lights out," 154
Logan (Mount), 7; *map*, 8
London, Jack, 82
Los Angeles, California, police department, 16
Loneliness, 23
Lucania (Mount), 29
McDermott, Granny, 174
Macdonald, Sir John A., 35–37
McIllree, Superintendent, 64–65

McKelvie, B. A., x
Mackenzie, Alexander, 10
Mackenzie (river), 4, 98–99, 117, 126
Mackenzie River (sternwheeler), 116, 126
McLean, R. D., ix
Macleod, James F., 41, 43, 46–49, 50, 51, 52, 53, 54, 55, 57, 59, 60, 78
Macleod (fort), 46, 51, 56–57; *map*, 8
McMurray (fort), 174; *map*, 8
MacNeil, R. A. S., ix, 157
McPherson (fort), 98–99, 102, 104, 107, 108; *map*, 8
Mail, 93, 98
Malaguer y Salvador, Don Miguel, 152–53
Malemutes, 23
Manitoba, 15, 38, 41, 161
Manning, Premier Ernest C., ix, 161
Maple Creek (post), 65; *map*, 8
Marleen (freighter), 152
Marriage, 25, 162
Marriages, recording of, 24
Mathewson, H. P., ix
Mercy, 163
Metis (half-breeds), 68–69
Military discipline, 154
Minnichinas Hills, 67
Mitkayout (woman), 24
Mine-sweepers, 152
Mistakes, 175
Montana, 50–51
Moodie, Inspector John, 31, 130
Moose, 5
Motor fuel (high-octane), 149
Motor Launch 16 (boat), 145
Motor vehicles, 151
Mountain Creek, 100, 101
Mukluks, 28, 117–18, 120, 121, 128
"Musical Ride," 172
Musk oxen, 5
Nahani Indian language, 24–25
Narcotics, 160
Native tongues, 23–24
Nechako River, 5–6
Nelson (fort), 156; *map*, 8

179

Index

New Brunswick, 161

Newfoundland, 142, 161

New York *Times*, 80

Nez Percé Indians, 54, 60

Night, northern, 138

Nichols, Graham, x

Nicholson, Leonard H., ix, 155–56

Norman (fort), 113, 116–17, 121

North Magnetic Pole, 124, 140, 142; *map*, 9

Northern Messenger (radio program), 138

Northern night, 138

Northern Pacific Railroad, 38, 41

Northwest Fur Company, 117

Northwest Mounted Police, 36, 52

Northwest Passage, route by water, 134–44

Northwest Service Command, 27

Nova Scotia, 161

O'Connor, James A., x, 13–14, 31, 129

Ottawa, Ontario, Canada; capital city, 11–12; confederation, 34; *map*, 9

Outlaws, 73–74

Oxen (musk), 5

Pacific Ocean, outlet, 64

Palugtok-angut, 114, 122–23

Parliament, 10

Parry, W. J., 136

Pasley Bay, 139

Peace River, 115, 116, 126–27, 129

Pearkes, General George R., 29–30

Peel River, 96, 104–07, 109

Pensions, 156

Perry, Commissioner, 128

Philadelphia, Pennsylvania, police, 16

Photography, 154

Physical requirements, 151

Pickpockets, 82

Pie-a-Pot, 65–67

Piegans, 33, 58–59

Piper, Aimee, 165–69, 173

Piper, Elizabeth Susan, 165, 169, 170, 173

Piper, John Fraser, ix, 165–69, 173

Piper, John MacDougall, 165, 169–70, 173

Piper, Storm, 91, 166, 170

Pitchblende, 7

Pleasant Camp, 88, 90

Police organizations, 25

Politics, 161

Pond Inlet, detachment, 22, 142; *map*, 9

Portland (steamer), 79

Potts, Jerry, 50

Prairie heat, 42–43

Prince Edward Island, 161

Prince George (town), 157; *map*, 8

Provincial police, 161

Provost Marshal, 155

Public relations, 157

Quarterly, 170

Queen's Birthday, 170

R. C. M. P. *See* Royal Canadian Mounted Police

Radford (explorer), 130

Radios, 138–39, 150, 162

Railroads, 54

Rampart House, 135

Radium (barge), 7

Red Crow (chief), 59

Regimental numbers, 169

Regina, Saskatchewan, 153, 155; *map*, 8

Reindeer, 5

Remounts, 172

Reports, 154

Revelstoke, 77–78; *map*, 8

Richardson Mountains, 135

Riel Rebellion, 68–69, 87

Rivett-Carnac, C. E., ix, 158–60

Robertson-Ross, Colonel Patrick, 36–37

Rockcliffe Barracks, 153, 163

Robson (Mount), 4

Rooke (carpenter), 94

Ross, Sir John, 140

Rouvier, Pierre (priest), 110–14, 117, 118, 119, 125, 126

Rouvier (lake), 119

Index

Rowed, Harry, ix
Royal Canadian Air Force, 151
Royal Canadian Mounted Police: authority, 14–15, 133, 160–61; Aviation Section, 151; books to read about, x; civilian character, 36; citizenship, 153; dogs, 151; duties, 19–21; educational requirements, 153; enlistment, 16; establishment, 12; explorations, 133, 134; horses, 146; insignia, 53, 60, 77; law, 19–20; Marine Division, 151–52; marksmanship, 20, 156–57; marriage, 25; modern crime detection methods, 146–50; motor vehicles, 151; motto, 12, 26, 44, 78, name change (*1904*), 91; name change (*1920*), 133; payroll, 15; physical requirements, 153; qualifications, 37; *Quarterly*, 170; salaries, 50, 156; scientific and mechanical equipment, 150–51; streamlined equipment, 158; training, 153–55; tunic, 150; uniform, 20, 50
Sabotage, 160
Saint Elias (Mount), 29; *map*, 8
Saint John (fort), 130; *map*, 8
Saint Mary (river), 32
Saint Roch (schooner), 134–44
Salaries, 37
Saskatchewan, 68, 74–75, 161
Saulte St. Marie, *map*, 9
Selkirk Mountain Range, 61, 64, 77
Sellon, Reverend, 88–90
Shooting, 157–58
Shoshone (cutter), 137
Silverman, Doctor, 30
Simmons, J. Aubrey, x
Simpson, Constable, 89
Single men, 25–26
Sinnisiak (guide), 110–14, 125, 126–27
Sioux Indians, 54–57
Sitting Bull (Sioux chief), 15–16, 54–57, 78
Skagway (port), 84, 87, 88
Skiffs, 152
Sled dogs. *See* Dog sleds

Smith, Jefferson ("Soapy"), 84, 87, 88
Smith (fort), 116
Smuggling, 152, 160
Snookum Jim, 33
Snow, 98
Snowshoes, 96–97
Snyder, Superintendent, 109
Solly, Sergeant, 145
Somers, Corporal, 101, 108
South Bloods, 59
Soviet spy ring, 153
Spanton, H. J., ix
Special Constables, 23
Spying, 160
Stamix Otokon, 53–55, 59–60
Steele, Superintendent, Sam, 63, 78, 82–83
Stefansson, Vilhjalmur, 117
Stevenson, Inspector Edward H., 149, 154
Stewart, Charlie, 109
"Stir crazy," 23
Street (explorer), 130
Supermen, 170–71
Swimming, 154
Taylor, Constable Richard, 99, 103–04, 107, 109
Tartar (steamer), 87, 88
Telegraph, 68, 91
Telephone, 150
Tenderfeet, 79–81
Terror (vessel), 11
Three Bulls (Indian), 49
Towill, George S., x
Toxicology, 154
Tradition, sense of, 155
Train robberies, 73–74
Treaty Day, 21, 58, 60
Tree River, 138
Trigger-happy recruits, 67
Tshimshean Indian Tribe, 145
Typewriting, 154
Uluksak (guide), 110, 113, 114, 125–27
Uniforms, 30–31, 36–37, 38–41
United Church of Canada, 169

Index

United States: area, 3; train robberies, 73; wildlife, 5

United States Cavalry, 53–54

Vancouver, British Columbia, 13–14, 63, 153–54, 160; *map*, 8; Northwest water route, 134–35, 144; railroad, 63

Vancouver Island, 145

Van Horne, Sir William, 70, 73

Van Norman, Constable, 22

Vincent, George G., ix

Victoria (Queen), 53, 57–58, 60

Victoria, British Columbia, 84

Victoria Island, 138

Victoria Land, 124

Victory (vessel), 140

"Vive La Compagnie" (song), 30

Walker Bay, 138

Walters, Constable, 63

Weakness, 125

Welsh, W. H., 93–94

Western Training Depot, Regina, 153, 155

Weyburn, Saskatchewan, 74–76; *map*, 8

Whisky trade, 32–36, 38, 41, 43, 45, 51, 52, 53, 59

Whitehorse (village), 82, 93, 149–50; *map*, 8

Whitehorse Rapids, 81

Whittaker, Reverend, 99

Wilson, Sergeant, 74

Witchcraft, 90

Wives, 162–63

Wood, Stuart Taylor, ix, 135–36, 155, 172

Wood, Zac, 83–88, 94, 136

Wrestling, 154

Yellowhead Pass, 69

Yellowknife, 173

Yiltcock (chief), 90

York boat, 117

Yukon (fort), 135; *map*, 8

Yukon (river), 4, 14, 81–82, 91–92, 98

Yukon Territory, 78–91, 149–50